Praise for J. Ruth Gendler's work~

"The very act of reading *Notes on the Need for Beauty* will change the way you see things. It will awaken you to notice beauty, to make beauty, to remember beauty. And this is a cause for celebration."
—Christiane Northrup, MD, author of *Mother-Daughter Wisdom*, *The Wisdom of Menopause*, and *Women's Bodies, Women's Wisdom*

"*Notes on the Need for Beauty* is delicious, a feast for the soul. Ruth Gendler's eye and heart are true and the vividness, constancy, and meticulousness of her meditation calls us to the banquet of beauty like music heard across a meadow. This is an utterly nuturing book, savory with loveliness from the exquisite cover art to the last morsel of wisdom."
—Tim Farrington, author of *The Monk Downstairs* and *Lizzie's War*

"Beauty is as beauty does and Ruth Gendler outdoes herself with this completely charming illustrated compilation of information and inspiration. *Notes on the Need for Beauty* is warm, winsome and very, very wise."
—Donna Henes, author of *The Queen of My Self*

"*Changing Light* makes two moves that are of absolute importance; it gives us an effective way to imagine daily life poetically, and it helps us be mindful of the cosmic rhythms and lighting that shape our lives— an ancient tradition that we've lost . . . I recommend spending at least a year with this little book."
—Thomas Moore, author of *Care of the Soul*

"The Qualities are wise and whimsical and express truth in a very personal way."

—Jean Bolen, author of *Goddesses in Every Woman*

"How I treasure this splendid collection of writings! Ruth Gendler must be one of those ancient mystical needleworkers, so skillfully has she selected these shimmering poems and luminous threads of prayers and songs and artwork and spun them for us into a precious cloth. I carry this with me when I travel, wrapping myself in it whenever I am distracted or tired, whenever I need to remember my interconnectedness in the weave of life."

—Sherry Ruth Anderson, author of *The Cultural Creatives*
and *The Feminine Face of God*

"In this time when we are losing our own senses by one percent per year, rediscovering the sense for beauty is an urgent priority that requires conscious employment. In *Notes on the Need for Beauty*, Ruth Gendler presents us with faceted seeds that can be planted in our own souls for rumination. She urges us to look at everything as aesthetic events, to not just look, but to look as if with our arms open. This book is a lighthouse of a gift for individual reimaginations for beauty wherever we uncover it."

—Paulus Berensohn, author of *Finding Your Way With Clay*

About the Author

J. Ruth Gendler is an artist, writer, and teacher. She is the author of *The Book of Qualities* and the editor of *Changing Light: The Eternal Cycle of Night and Day*. *The Book of Qualities*, now in its fortieth printing, has been adapted as a two-act theater piece and translated into German, Japanese, and Chinese. In addition to personal essays and poems, Gendler writes about the arts, education, health, and books. Her artwork has been exhibited nationally. Gendler has taught writing and art in a variety of settings for twenty years. She has been an artist in residence with both California Poets in the Schools and Young Audiences of the Bay Area, and leads writing and creativity workshops. She received her BA in English and communications from Stanford University, and she now resides in Berkeley, California. Her website is: www.ruthgendler.com.

Also by the Author

The Book of Qualities
Changing Light

Notes on the Need for Beauty

An Intimate Look at an Essential Quality

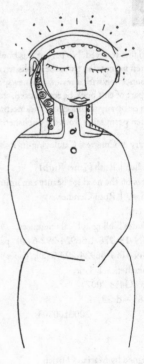

J. Ruth Gendler

with drawings by the author

Marlowe & Company
New York

NOTES ON THE NEED FOR BEAUTY: *An Intimate Look at an Essential Quality*

Copyright © 2007 by J. Ruth Gendler
Copyright © 2007 Drawings by J. Ruth Gendler

Published by
Marlowe & Company
An Imprint of Avalon Publishing Group, Incorporated
245 West 17th Street • 11th Floor
New York, NY 10011-5300

AVALON

Library of Congress Cataloging-in-Publication Data

Gendler, J. Ruth (Janet Ruth)
Notes on the need for beauty : an intimate look at an essential
quality / J. Ruth Gendler.
   p. cm.
Includes bibliographical references.
ISBN-13: 978-1-56924-292-6 (alk. paper)
ISBN-10: 1-56924-292-5 (alk. paper)
1. Aesthetics. I. Title.
BH39.G453 2007
111'.85—dc22
            2006100103

Designed by Marian O'Brien
Production by jcampstudio.com

In honor of my mother

and

In memory of my father

Contents

Notes on the Need for Beauty

Invitation to Beauty

B eauty doesn't mind questions and she is fond of riddles. Beauty will dance with anyone who is brave enough to ask her. When I first wrote these words twenty-five years ago, I had only begun to imagine how we could invite beauty into our lives. I had no idea how deeply they would lead me into an exploration of beauty.

Writing about beauty feels like drinking water out of the cup of my hand from a clear spring. As I bring this water to my mouth, so much spills away. The water tastes delicious; the freshness and purity startle me. I have been drinking water that was mediocre for so long, I have forgotten how good water can taste. Like water, beauty is ordinary and essential, as well as extraordinary and magnificent.

Beauty, like water, takes many forms and permeates our environment. Just as water travels across the world and pools in everything from our cells to underground streams to magnificent storms, beauty also travels, gathers, concentrates. It is beautiful to look at and listen to the way the world changes with rain, to trace the path of the river by foot or from an airplane window, to talk at the ocean's edge, swim under the waterfall. Beauty rinses our eyes. Sometimes beauty moves us to tears. We bathe in, drink the presence of beauty.

Slowly I have come to savor the beauty of the unknown, the unnameable, the contradictions and paradoxes. Beauty is simple and complex, obvious and elusive, superficial and profound, spontaneous and achieved with great effort, impossible to define and essential to articulate.

Beauty is allied with the radiance of fire, body and soul, vision and music, movement and stillness, the daily cycles of night and day.

Beauty refuses to yield to analysis, refuses to be perfection. Beauty moves within and around us, rearranging our moods, taking us home. Beauty is always moving and beauty is very still, the light in the dark, the dark in the light, the subtlest shades of pale white and blue, the richest tones of indigo and black and deep brown, the brightest reds and oranges and golds. We find beauty at the intersections, the edges, the center of so many experiences. Although we keep trying to talk about beauty as inner or outer, that language is too static, trying to fix beauty in a single location. Beauty is an energy, not an image, and that energy can go anywhere; that energy takes on an image, a form, many images, many forms.

As a visual artist, I tend to think about beauty in visual terms, though making art that is beautiful is rarely my conscious intent. Making art is a practice of seeing, and as we see more deeply, we find beauty in unexpected places. When I make art, I slow down and my perceptions of the things around me are heightened. The feel of the paper, the three new jars of blue paints, the shiny black ink, the textures and liveliness of the materials are in themselves satisfying. Sometimes when I emerge from my studio, everything that was ordinary becomes so vivid that it stuns me. Although I have never been stopped for speeding, I was once pulled over for driving too slowly; there was simply so much to see.

Being an artist has offered me a way to practice developing my vision and to work with the knowing of the senses; my hands know how to make order, how to place one stone next to another stone as if it were a language. Making art is part of how I make sense, how I see my experience. I begin to draw people with leaves in their hearts; to my amazement the leaf people begin to look like angels. A shape turns into other shapes. Leaf becomes flame becomes wing.

My work has involved looking at the familiar in new ways, allowing myself to be led by my questions, listening to the dreams and stories of my friends, teachers, and students. The normal activities of my life become part of the way I take notes on the need for beauty. Living on a lake and watching the sun rise over the water for a week, talking to second graders about the animals in their dreams, visiting gardens and salvage yards, adding a third window in my office and bringing more light inside, become opportunities to explore different qualities of beauty.

Writing about beauty feels like swimming in a Sierra lake after years of doing laps in an indoor pool. There is a freedom to swimming in a mountain lake that is exhilarating. Swimming for joy, I feel the great depth of water beneath me and the sky above me, and my creature self comes alive. I may not see the trout or otter I share the water with, but I know I am not alone.

The research has truly been a search on many levels. I yearned to look outside the jacket of my conditioning to cultures in which the Mystery is alive, in which there is more time devoted to celebration, exchanging gifts, dancing, making music. Although I wanted to travel to faraway places, I found some of my most important travels were as an artist and poet in the schools. Listening to children consider beauty and ugliness underlined that beauty is, in fact, everywhere. On my very first visit to a classroom, an adolescent boy wrote, "Beauty doesn't drink Perrier water. Beauty doesn't eat finger sandwiches with her afternoon tea. Beauty doesn't wear a lacy nightie. For Beauty is too busy tending the rice fields in China."

I am not researching beauty to prove an academic argument; I don't have a single vision or theory. I am exploring and celebrating beauty, feeling that beauty is both precious and common, far too absent in our culture and everyday life and yet very available when we give our attention over to it. Because so much of our culture focuses on its most superficial aspects, we have forgotten that beauty is one of the most profound and essential qualities in our lives. I have come to believe that by attending to beauty and enlarging our sense of beauty, we are able to live with greater appreciation, engagement, wonder, and reverence.

When I was younger, I couldn't sort out all the different qualities of beauty. I often wanted to distance myself from what I considered our culture's superficial emphasis on appearances. Equating beauty with something fancy and inaccessible didn't make sense with my experience of the abundance of beauty. I was fascinated with what happens when one brings a small piece of nature inside—a shell, a feather, an unidentified white flower—and how these intimate gestures change and charge a space.

At the end of my freshman year in college some friends and I made the odyssey crosscountry in a small stuffed Toyota. I most remember a night in June in western Nebraska. As I watched the sun set and a full moon rise over the small green hills, I sensed a fragrance of wholeness, of holiness that the prayer books had hinted at. On that ribbon of road the sky came all the way to the ground. There was such a big space to see the light change. Looking back now, that may have been the first time I recognized that for me, beauty is intimately linked with the immense rhythms of time and light.

In my twenties, in an effort to be a serious person, I acted as if beauty were unimportant or overrated. At the same time I was often dismayed by the ugliness I saw around me. When I began to write articles about craftspeople, I was drawn not only to their finished work, but to the process of making something sensual and essential. I felt happier in the spaces where they worked, delighted by the attention to texture, the intelligence in the hand. Weavers spinning yarn in rich and muted tones, textile artists with their shelves of fabrics arranged by color, all spoke of the beauty of ordinary things.

During this time I sketched out the first few pages of "notes on the need for beauty" mostly as a lament for the many ways I saw beauty being distorted, misunderstood, and manipulated. Now I trust that beauty is far too important a quality to leave to the image-makers in advertising, fashion, cosmetics, magazines, movies.

I remember when Anne Herbert's phrase "Practice random kindness and senseless acts of beauty" first appeared and how quickly it caught on. This simple imperative told us to be generous and creative, skillful and surprising. It delighted people because it linked beauty with kindness, taking beauty beyond the realm of aesthetics and bringing it home to the heart; it was both practical and ethical advice. Beauty breaks us open and connects us to the hearts of others, the soul of the world, deepens our connections with the places we live and dream about, the people we love, animals and plants, trees and rivers. Beauty opens the door to creativity and wisdom.

Perhaps we trivialize beauty because we know it is powerful. Beauty stops us in our tracks, takes us outside of ourselves at the same time it brings us into ourselves. Often we are jaded because we have not tasted its true sweetness. What is called "heartful" is often soft and sticky, lacking the clarity, focus, audacity, and fierceness that the true heart insists on, that beauty carries. We live cut off from the beauty of the living earth, cut off from the beauty inside us. How can we know what real sweetness is when we live in a time and place that has moved so far away from what is essential?

When I discuss the quality of beauty with students, we imagine beauty's relationships with curiosity and courage, fear, ugliness, and harmony. Curiosity, like beauty, becomes a name for the desire that draws things out of themselves, toward each other. "The river is curious to get to the ocean. The ocean is curious to meet the river," a girl begins her poem, describing how curiosity, like beauty, brings us closer to the mysteries at the heart of nature. "Curiosity taught the kitten to walk, the river to run, the flowers to bloom," a sixth grade boy declares, and it echoes psychologist James Hillman's statement that beauty is the way "in which the gods touch our senses, reach the heart and attract us into life." Hillman's definition doesn't say what beauty is, but suggests how it moves us into the world. Beauty is not accidental, frivolous, or marginal, but at the very center, stirring our hearts and our sensitive, sensuous bodies, attracting us into life with its immediacy and delight.

Contemporary scientists are beginning to document what native cultures and ancient scientists have long held true: there is a sacred pattern, a hidden wholeness, a harmony that underlies everything. When traditional peoples speak of the Beauty Road, there is a great respect for balance, the balance between night and day, earth and sky, masculine and feminine, life and death. In contrast to the idea that beauty is transient and rare, there is the possibility that beauty is our most natural relationship to life. In the Taoist symbolism of yin and yang, in the sacred mandalas of Tibetan monks, in Aboriginal dreamtime, in the Celtic alphabet, there is an honoring of the rhythms and patterns, the beauty, wisdom, and power of nature.

The Navajo word *hozho*, translated into English as "beauty," also means harmony, wholeness, goodness. One story that suggests the dynamic way that beauty comes alive between us concerns a contemporary Navajo weaver. "A man ordered a rug of an especially complex pattern on two separate occasions from the same weaver. Both rugs came out perfectly, and the weaver remarked to her brother that there must have been something special about the owner. It was understood that the outcome of the rugs was dependent not on the weaver's skill and ability but upon the *hozho* in the owner's life. The *hozho* of his life evoked the beauty in the rugs." In the Navajo worldview, beauty exists not simply in the object, or in the artist who made the object; it is expressed in relationships.

Although we live in a highly materialistic culture, paradoxically we don't care very much about things, what they are made from, how we are when we are making them. As the potter Carla Needleman said, "We take in with the bread the attitude of the baker." Thomas Merton said, "The peculiar grace of a Shaker chair is due to the fact that it was made by someone capable of believing that an angel might come and sit in it."

Beauty is a presence and a friend, a teacher, a companion, the guest who visits unannounced, the guest you wish would stay longer. In our own lives, filled with our aches and yearnings, we often take beauty for granted. In the reports of people living in the most extreme conditions, we hear testaments to the sustaining power of beauty. During the Nazi occupation of Belgium, René Magritte, known for his ironic and intelligent surrealist style, found himself making lush Impressionist paintings as a way to affirm and celebrate life amid the horrors of his time.

As a child growing up in Maoist China, Jung Chang's family was sent from the cement compound to a beautiful old apartment on the top floor of a three-story house. "In those days, beauty was so despised that my family was sent to this lovely house as a punishment. The main room was big and rectangular, with a parquet floor. Three sides were glass which made it brilliantly light and on a clear day offered a panoramic view of the distant snowy mountains." Both the expansive view and the simple play of sunlight and moonlight, leaf and shadow, brought happiness to Chang. "On a calm night, lying in bed with the moonlight filtering through the windows, and the shadow of the tall paper mulberry tree dancing on the wall, I was filled with joy."

Living in a time of well-documented crisis—environmental, educational, social—we are often numb and overwhelmed by what's wrong, what's ugly, what's out of balance. The healing we need as individuals and cultures cannot come only from practical solutions and prescriptions, but must also come from many visions of wholeness, holiness, visions of beauty. We must take the time to discover what is beautiful to each of us, beautiful enough that we are willing to protect and cherish it, change our lives; beautiful in the indigenous sense that it is beauty that organizes and gives meaning and purpose to the world.

The ability to perceive, to respond, to create beauty is a triumph against brutality and, also, mediocrity. Beauty is like a medicine made from local herbs that steadies and strengthens, tonifies the nervous system. A friend who moved to the California coast notes, "Living here surrounded by beauty, for the first time in my life my inner landscape is supported by the external landscape. I feel so much more at peace."

This book invites you to expand and deepen your own sense of beauty. It honors beauty as a quality that is both substantial and spiritual, one that exists within, between, and among us. I want to celebrate what's beautiful to me: the human face, body and spirit, language, light and color, life rhythms, nature, many kinds of art. I am making a plea in our efficient, speed-driven society to slow down, to reflect, to engage the senses, the eyes and hands, the sense of wonder. One of the reasons we don't experience beauty is because we are moving too fast to keep our senses and our hearts open to what is around us. Beauty reveals itself over time, and we lose much of the beauty available to us when we get ahead of ourselves.

The title *Notes on the Need for Beauty* embodies the essence of the book, conveying the sense that these are thoughts, stories, reflections, lyrical explorations that spiral around the quality of beauty. "Notes" suggests the language of music. "Need for Beauty" because we have forgotten how beauty gives meaning and purpose to our lives. Beauty brings us home to the ordinary, earthy, earthly sacred; it nourishes, renews, disturbs, comforts, and wakes us up. Beauty is revealed through attention, and by paying attention to the particulars, we discover the immense variety of ways that beauty shines forth in our lives, the extraordinary ways that beauty is rooted in soul.

Notes on the Need for Beauty grew out of conversations with gardeners and architects, dancers and teachers, beauticians, therapists, and scientists. Listening to people's stories about tattoos and watches, maple trees and makeup, favorite clothes and travels, beauty secrets and love stories, I hear how beauty is part of everyday life, part of our nature, part of our environment. And it is in the spirit of a conversation that it is offered, a conversation that travels and returns, circles, pauses, hums, and invites further conversations.

As a writer and artist, I speak two similar but distinct languages. I don't write books as much as I make them, and part of the pleasure of creating this book has been the exchange between words and pictures. It's not that the words illustrate the pictures or the images explain the text, but they inspire, echo, and refer to each other. At times I have regarded my art as play and my writing as work, but in fact both art and writing are work and play. And as serious as I am about the importance of beauty, it has been absolutely essential to bring a sense of play and delight to this subject. My intention is that the text and drawings invite you to read at your own rhythm and pace, to reflect and consider your own experience of beauty.

Our willingness to see and honor beauty makes more beauty possible. Beauty, like every other quality—courage, fear, ugliness, trust, truth, wisdom—is a part of us and apart from us, inside us and outside us, personal and impersonal. Beauty invites us to build bridges and make connections between the senses and the soul, between contemplation and expression, between ourselves and the world.

Aphrodite's Gift

I am so small I can barely be seen.
How can this great love be inside of me?

Look at your eyes. They are small
but they see enormous things.

Rumi
translated by Coleman Barks

Who gave you your eyes?

This is one of my favorite questions. As I take notes on the need for beauty I want to consider how you and I see the world. I can't know how you see the world, so I ask you, "Who gave you your eyes?" Inside this question are several other questions. Who taught you to see? Who taught you *what* to see? What not to see? What are you paying attention to? What is beautiful to you?

We see in the light and in the dark. We see before we can speak. We see with our eyes closed. We see in our dreams. We see much more than we can ever say. I remember someone showing me how to tie my shoelaces, how to drive, how to tear paper with a straight edge, but I can't remember not seeing and someone showing me how to see.

We can't see ourselves.

We can't see ourselves whole. We can see our hands stretched out in front of us, we can bend our heads down and view the rest of the front of our bodies; we can turn our heads over a shoulder and see the line of

13

a leg. We need a mirror to look at our own faces. We need a mirror to begin to see our full selves, our bodies from head to toe, all together, not just parts. We need two mirrors to see what our backs look like.

A traveler tells me that we live in each other's gaze. We depend on each other to see ourselves. And yet we must also cultivate the courage to look at ourselves as we are. It is a tremendous work to see for ourselves, not just to accept what others see, but to be who we really are, to develop our own vision.

We are taught what to see, what not to see, when we are so young we rarely remember or investigate the choices involved. I makes lists of five things I see, five things I don't see, five things I want to see, trying to expand my capacity to envision, visualize, to observe more precisely, to imagine more completely, to see with more awareness and fewer ideas about what I am seeing. I see how the pink-purple of the magnolia flowers echoes the blue-violet of the lilac. I don't see the way my shoulders pull in when I'm asthmatic. I see the early morning fog. I don't see the moon during the day. I want to see the light around your eyes.

When we are able to say what we see, do we see it more clearly or do we stop looking as carefully? When we are able to say what we don't see, are we able to see it, imagine it, wonder about it? To become conscious of *what* we see is a beginning, a way to acknowledge that we have learned to see and can learn to see more. To become more conscious of *how* we see is to know our selves and our tendencies, our prejudices, our outlooks. Driving in the car one day I hear a report on the radio about a British scientist who studied people who had suffered strokes and were only able to report seeing one thing at a time—a fork, or a spoon, or a plate. Actually, when questioned further, they "saw" more than they knew they had. How often those of us with unimpaired sight concentrate on only one thing and can't see what's around it.

In *Catching the Light*, the physicist Arthur Zajonc recounts the story of a boy, blind from birth, whose eyes were operated on by surgeons. After the bandages were removed, his doctors waved a hand in front of the child's eyes and asked him what he saw. "He replied weakly, 'I don't know.' . . . The boy's eyes were clearly not following the slowly moving hand. What he saw was only a varying brightness in front of him. He was then allowed to touch the hand as it began to move; he cried out in a voice of triumph: 'It's moving!' He could feel it move, and even, as he said, 'hear it move,' but he still needed laboriously to learn to see it move. Light and eyes were not enough to grant him sight. Passing through the now-clear black pupil of the child's eye, that first light called forth no echoing image from within. The child's sight began as a hollow, silent, dark, and frightening kind of seeing. The light of day beckoned, but no light of mind replied within the boy's anxious, open eyes."

We learn to see in relationship to ourselves, our loved ones, the world around us. We learn to see, touch, taste the world at the same time. Infants study shadows, candle flames, faces. Mothers note the infinite space in babies' eyes. Fathers speak of the experience of loving and being loved as their babies look at them with open, adoring eyes, taking in everything. A friend calls it "baby gazing"—the tender and compelling, deeply generous exchange as parent and child investigate each other's souls. In babies' eyes nothing is absent or hidden.

The peekaboo of mother and baby becomes the hide-and-seek of neighborhood children, siblings. The little girl shouts gleefully, "Look at me, don't look at me. You can't see me." Throughout our lives we negotiate between wanting to hide and wanting to be seen. The experience of seeing and being seen at the same time is alternately terrifying and beautiful. Often, in these moments, we know ourselves both as whole and complete in ourselves and wholly, completely part of the world. We belong to ourselves and to each other. We live in each other's gaze.

We hear the linking of our identity and our vision in the very sounds of our language. Who I am comes out of what "eye" has seen. As we use that first-person singular pronoun, *I*, the second *eye* seems to run up from behind. The *yes* in *eyes*, the seeing in the Spanish yes, *si*.

I have always been moved by a scene in the John Sayles movie *The Brother from Another Planet* in which the Brother removes his eye and hands it to the drug lord, who is comfortably distanced from the chaos of the street in his tall office building. The eyeball is filled with the scenes of pain that the interplanetary visitor has observed. In a science fiction movie it's possible to make the impulse to share one's vision explicit. It is a powerful, poetic, political rendering of the idea of giving someone your eyes.

Insight/Outlook: The Language of Vision

Sight leads us to insight. A lookout is a position to look from, where we can see all around us for a great distance. From looking out we develop an outlook, a point of view, a perspective, a way of looking out past what we see to the unknowable future.

Seeing occurs up close and at a distance. We can be near- or farsighted, focused on close looking, inner images, or external phenomena. When we spend too much time looking at things up close, we strain our eyes. Native peoples have known about the importance of the "long view." Seeing the distance gives us perspective. Seeing the distance opens the heart.

Seeing is one of our primary ways of knowing. Both *theory* and *theater* are derived from the Greek *thea*, the act of looking. A *theater* is a place for looking at something; a *theory* looks at a set of facts and sees their relationship. I like the old word *behold*. Because the *holding* in *behold* suggests touch, touching with the eyes.

There are so many different ways to see, choices of direction, not just near and far, into and beyond, around and through, with detachment and engagement, disinterest, reverence, affection, and awe. We can glance or glimpse quickly or scrutinize, examine or observe for a long time. Practice looking at something closely, then close your eyes and feel what you have just looked at and then open your eyes and look again. Each looking is a different seeing.

Emotional qualities inform our vision. We gaze with tenderness or stare warily. Gawk, wink, glare in anger, watch impatiently, or regard with great curiosity. We can be passionately involved with what we are seeing—"I'm willing to see you through this"—or detached and observant—"Let's see what happens." It is a great task to see with both compassion and detachment simultaneously. We can focus on the surface or see with the eye of the heart to the inside. A visionary sees what is and sees through what is to what could be.

We have the capacity to look in and look out much like we breathe in and breathe out. Look into the world of intuition and imagination, energy, visions, and dreams. Light shimmers around the edges, and what looks solid and familiar is revealed as spinning, whirling, dancing. It is beautiful to explore the play between what we bring our eyes to look at and what comes to our eyes when we allow them to receive.

We have heard the expression "Beauty is in the eye of the beholder" so often we don't deepen into what it means. Yet as we grow older, certain experiences startle us, pull the wool away from our eyes. We "sort of know" that others see the world differently than we do and that our beliefs are shaping what we see. Although we see each other, we don't see what or how the other sees. Humbly, tentatively, and with frustration and love, we speak about how we see things—to begin to know each other's lives and points of view, to begin to appreciate each other's insights and outlooks. We say, "Perhaps, I am not *seeing* all there is. Perhaps I need to *see* it your way. Maybe there is more here than meets the eye."

In his autobiography, *An Anthropology of Everyday Life*, anthropologist Edward Hall quotes a friend, "What you see, is what you intend to do about it." This is a profoundly simple statement about the ways we limit our vision. How many things we can't let ourselves see because we can't do anything about them: things that need mending, repairing, repainting, suffering, ugliness. What we pretend not to see doesn't go away (where would it go?), but we do. As we cut ourselves off from ugliness, things that are painful to look at, we also cut ourselves off from beauty. It takes courage to start to look at what we do not see, to be willing to see with more curiosity and less certainty.

The language of sight is a language of faith and doubt, wariness, watchfulness, and wonder. In *Oh, What a Blow That Phantom Gave Me!* anthropologist Edmund Carpenter writes, "It's not easy to experience the unfamiliar, the unnamed. We say, 'If I hadn't seen it with my own eyes, I wouldn't have believed it,' but the phrase really should be, 'If I hadn't believed it with all my heart, I wouldn't have seen it.'"

Seeing changes us. Seeing more, we are more alive. Being alive, we are constantly seeing new things. We sightsee, traveling both to feed our eyes new sights and to return home and see the familiar with fresh eyes. You might say that the greater challenge is to see what is familiar, but traveling, a change of scene, the shock of breaking routine, works to wake and shake us up so that when we return, the familiar becomes a bit stranger.

Wit, *wisdom*, and *visit* share the Latin root *videre*, to see. Other words that contain seeing in their center include *evidence* and *envy*; *perspective*, *introspection*, and *spectacle*; *admiration*, *mirage*, and *miracle*, *provision* and *revision*. We have *inspectors* who look into things, and *spectators* and *onlookers* who fill up our stadiums. I wish we had more "respectors"; praising the beauty we overlook, a respector looks and looks again.

How do people whose jobs depend on their looking, gardeners who work on the same site for years, classroom teachers who are with the same children every day, keep their seeing fresh, so they are seeing moment to moment rather than relying on what they have seen before? Perhaps there is a clue in the prepositions that accompany the verbs of seeing. Their precision offers us a place to position and aim our sight. Watch how the word *look* becomes more focused as it is paired with various prepositions—at, for, into, out, down, up, over, forward. At the same time that these prepositions provide a specific direction for the eyes, they remind us of the metaphoric nature of seeing, as well. Looking forward takes our eyes out in front of us into the future. By literally moving our eyes, experimenting with direction and focus, we experience new ways of seeing.

Although I have been most curious about the differences between looking in and looking out, there are so many choices of where and how to look. When I look at you, you become a place for me to see, a landscape with many regions, familiar and unknown. There are so many ways to see you.

Eyes of Imagination, Observation, Wonder & Love

Among twenty snowy mountains,
The only moving thing
Was the eye of the blackbird.

Wallace Stevens

In a brief, beautiful essay, "Horizontal Grandeur," Minnesota writer Bill Holm distinguishes between two ways of seeing, which he calls "the prairie eye" and "the woods eye." "The prairie eye looks for distance, clarity, and light; the woods eye for closeness, complexity, and darkness. The prairie eye looks for usefulness and plainness in art and architecture; the woods eye for the baroque and ornamental."

Holm describes how someone with a woods eye looks at twenty miles of prairie and sees nothing but grass. The one with a prairie eye "looks at a square foot and sees a universe; ten or twenty flowers and grasses, heights, heads, colors, shades, configurations, bearded, rough, smooth, simple, elegant. When a cloud passes over the sun, colors shift, like a child's kaleidoscope ... Trust a prairie eye to find beauty and understate it truthfully, no matter how violent the apparent exaggeration. Thoreau, though a woodsman, said it right: 'I can never exaggerate enough.'"

Translating Holm's images of the two kinds of eyes into my language, I think about the night eye and the day eye, the eye of the dreamer and the eye of the builder, the eye of observation and the eye of imagination.

The writer Elizabeth Rose Campbell once described the imagination as the foot soldier of the soul, the source of everything, the beginning and end point. "Imagination can never go bankrupt, but it can become distorted, if we take on other people's dreams as our own ... To know who we are, we must have honest conversations, the imagination present often. We do this in waking dreams and sleeping dreams. And we do this through art and poetry, which is not some magical moment given to the rare few. It is the quiet companion of a long steady afternoon of losing one's self, letting go of who you think you are so you can remember who you are."

Nothing happens that we don't imagine. What we imagine is a kind of inner/outer seeing; it comes in before it goes out. The eye of the imagination is the eye of the heart looking into the secrets of the soul, illuminating the hidden sources of beauty, then looking out toward the edge of vision. The eye of the imagination is the eye of empathy, imagining what the world looks like to another person, imagining that the things in this world are looking back at us. It is the eye of coherence connecting the parts into a whole, the past to the future, juxtaposing colors and textures to design an outfit, a room, a garden.

I asked my niece when she was ten if Hawaii was the most beautiful place she had ever been, and she answered promptly, "No, my imagination is." To her it was obvious that the imagination is much more immense and beautiful than any one place. A sixth grader writes, "I think Imagination lives in a garden of roses and every time a flower blooms, a new idea is born," creating a link between the outer world and the inner world, between a thought and a flower. Although we usually focus on the imagination as a source of mental pictures, the imagination has physical, emotional, and spiritual aspects. At this time when we are drowning in images from the media, it is more important than ever to know our own images, to celebrate and cultivate the eye of the imagination.

The eye of the imagination enlarges our ideas of beauty. It is the ecstatic eye of the mystic Rumi telling us, "It is time to speak of roses and pomegranates, and of the ocean where the pearls are made of language and vision and of the invisible ladders which are different for each person that lead to the infinite places where trees murmur among themselves."

Because by nature I readily identify with the eye of the imagination, I have been deeply moved by exercises that strengthen the eye of observation. When I consider the question "Who gave me my eyes?" I think of the teachers who showed me how to observe things in the world around us with more care and precision. Whether they intended it or not, their instructions led me to beauty.

My high school chemistry teacher asked us to spend a few minutes gazing at a candle flame and then describe it in a paragraph. It is simple to look at something as ordinary as a flame and write down what you see in front of you. Yet, no one in the entire class of thirty-four students mentioned the dark blue cone at the core of the light. Why didn't we mention the blue? Because we expected something that gives off heat and light to be yellow and red. Because we had seen it so many times we hadn't noticed it. Because we had seen it so many times, it didn't seem important.

Now I often light candles during the day when I work to mark the time I am giving to the work, to strengthen my intention, to experience companionship in solitude, to be reminded of the beauty of light. This small flame speaks of the steadiness of burning, the pleasure of watching the fire dance; it offers clarity and encouragement. Time measured by candles. How long did it take to write this chapter? Nine candles.

Looking at a candle flame is not only an act of observation; it contains the seeds of inspiration, contemplation, and imagination. The candle flame links us to all kinds of fire—the fiery eye of the sun that makes our lives possible, the hidden fire at the heart of the earth under crust and mantle, the fire in the heart. The candle flame also suggests the spiritual nature of vision. I remember my mother telling me when I was young that during the darkest days of World War II, Eleanor Roosevelt said, "It is better to light a single candle than to curse the darkness." Each of us is a candle waiting to be kindled, lit, and consecrated. We are lit from within, and sometimes the light pours out of us.

A few years after writing about the candle flame, I was at a nature drawing workshop at the Point Reyes National Seashore and the instructor asked us to draw a picture of a daisy. After we finished our drawings, he handed each of us a daisy to examine and draw again.

I will never forget the contrast between our tidy and symmetrical first drawings—identical petals, perfectly round centers, vague leaves—and the second ones made when we really looked at daisies as we drew them. All the admonitions to be specific are unnecessary when we encounter one real anything. So this is a daisy leaf, a daisy calyx, a daisy petal, irregular, particular, itself. Drawing becomes an act of regard, respect, reverence.

I don't know what I am seeing until I draw. When we study what we love to see, we don't need to analyze it coldly. We can grow in wonder even as we deepen our understanding. Watching the sunset with a physicist, he tells me about the cross sections of dust particles scattering in the atmosphere, which is why the light colors are changing from pink to red to light blue-violet. The sunset is no less beautiful because my friend is explaining the technical aspects of the colors.

Henry David Thoreau, standing for hours beside a pond to observe young frogs, or all day at river's edge observing duck eggs hatching, noted, "I have a commonplace book for facts, and another for poetry, but I find it difficult always to preserve the vague distinction which I had in mind, for the most interesting and beautiful facts are so much the more poetry and that is their success. They are translated from earth to heaven. I see that if my facts were sufficiently vital and significant—perhaps transmuted into the substance of the human mind—I should need but one book of poetry to contain them all." Thoreau's statement points to the place where knowledge and love intersect, where the common facts of our world—tide charts and moon risings, pictures of flowers and descriptions of trees, recipes and maps—become the images of our poetry, where natural history and personal history become the sources of wisdom and beauty.

To me the candle flame and the daisy and the eye that sees them belong to the book of wonders and to the book of facts. Studying how the eye works, like studying the candle flame and the flower, is an exercise in contemplating the beautiful. The biology of vision is full of beautiful facts—perhaps because the eye is an extension of the brain and the only visible part of the nervous system. Even in technical discussions about the eye, the descriptions are filled with unintentional poetry. The eye "harvests" light and "translates light into electricity." The retina is "woven of brain cells."

The retina is a net catching light, a thin red membrane made of three distinct layers of nerve cells. These light-sensitive cells translate the image into a pattern of nerve impulses that travel along the optic nerve to the brain. Within the retina the nerve cells are intricately interconnected. Some cells sense spots, others respond to lines, others to movement. The long, thin rods work in dim light and see gradations. In contrast, the cones work in bright light, react quickly, and see in great detail and in color. In each human eye there are about 125 million rods and 7 million cones. The eye sends 1 billion pieces of information to the brain every second.

It's hard for me to wrap my mind around large numbers, so I can't quite imagine all these tiny light-sensitive cells. Everyone in New York City, as one cone in the eye of New York. Although I know there are a lot fewer rods and cones in the eye than stars in the sky (100 billion galaxies, each with about a billion stars) something about these tiny cells perceiving light reminds me of the distant stars. Both the tiny and the distant seem miraculous. Our eyes give us the universe, enable us to sense what is out there and bring it inside. We can't smell the stars or taste the stars or touch the stars, but we can see their light.

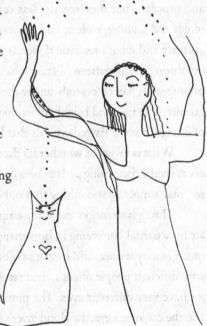

The diversity of eyes among animals is also beautiful. When we consider the different kinds of seeing required of owls and eels, sea horses and snakes, hunters and herbivores, this diversity makes sense. Eyes are structured for different kinds of environments. Color-blind owls see in dim light and darkness; their eyes amplify their hearing. Cats' eyes seem to glow in the dark, because their retinas have a mirrorlike lining. The sea horse swims upright with swiveling eyes; elusive flies with five eyes, three simple and two complex, see us, thousands of small images of us, faster than we can see them. "The eagle eye" is not just a metaphor; many birds have the ability to see far more acutely than we do. The eagle's eyes give her a form of monocular vision to see different things with each eye, as well as the capacity to shift to the binocular vision that we have. Telescopic vision enables the eagle to see her prey when she's flying high above the earth. With dual focusing power, the eagle sees at a distance in one moment and at closer range the next.

The more I study and imagine how people and animals see the world and process what they see, the less certain I am about what the words *visible* and *invisible, realistic* and *abstract, beautiful* and *ugly* mean. What's abstract and what's realistic depends on the kind of lens you are looking through. The pattern of stars looks like an electron map. A physicist photographs flawed crystals under the microscope, and with their crisp, geometric shapes and bright colors they look like contemporary abstract paintings. It is the flawed crystals that have the beautiful forms.

What is invisible, whether it's the ultraviolet patterns on white flowers as vivid as launching pads to bees or the heat of the infrared that snakes see, may simply be something that our eyes are not structured to see.

Through attention and study, empathy and imagination, we appreciate how partial our seeing is, how many other ways there are to see, how much beauty we see, and how much beauty we don't see. Taking a walk with different people offers a vivid reminder that by training and affinity we have very different eyes. The prairie eye and the forest eye, yes, but also the cat lover's eye, the cloud lover's eye, the eye that notices doors and windows, the oak and alder eye, the suspicious eye, the generous eye.

Walking in a familiar place with a new friend, walking in a new place with an old friend, walking with young children (is it because they are so close to the ground that they are willing to stop, explore, sniff out so much more than the rest of us?) I am always surprised by what we say to each other and see together. I hike with an old friend in the Colorado mountains as she identifies wildflowers, reads evidence of elk in the grass, talks about her recent trip to Tibet. The words come not just from us talking, but from our being together in this place. My friends, with their vision and their language, enlarge my world, help me see beauty, give me my eyes.

My eye changes according to what is on my mind. Walking around my neighborhood on an early Sunday morning while I'm anticipating taking down an awkward fence that breaks up my backyard, I see all kinds of fences—short wooden fences that mark a line but don't block the view, modern chain-link fences opposite beautifully weathered gray-brown fences, tired old falling-down fences next to young, cheerful fences, rough logs on the same street with sharp white pickets.

I didn't realize that fences could be so eloquent, awkward, charming, beautiful. I see how the same fence is repeated around the neighborhood to such different effects, left bare, painted red, painted green, white, or weathered. I see the way people's fences do or don't look like their houses, and then I watch the people come out of their houses, the way their houses do or do not resemble them. During the walks I take after my fence is down, I've stopped looking at fences, I'm focusing on studying the shadows of flowers and trees, the play between rocks and grasses. And then at different ways to construct a stone path.

To practice seeing more carefully is a wonderful assignment. To attempt to see more purely, to practice seeing out of one's own eyes. Alternate close observation and big imagining. Take a walk, and immediately afterward record ten images in words, in energetic sketches. Take a walk and imagine what someone else looks at, how someone else sees, what a cat notices, what a hawk focuses on, what a tree standing still in the same place knows.

The eyes feed the mind. Sometimes we try so hard to "change our minds," to not think certain thoughts. One of the most overlooked ways to change one's mind is to attend to what one looks at, to practice feeding one's eyes. To "change your mind," to interrupt anxiety or to practice gratitude or notice more beauty, pay attention to what you are literally looking at. Is it feeding the part of you that wants to be fed?

See where you are, not so much to locate yourself emotionally but physically. What are you looking at? Observe yourself in your surroundings. See who you are in this place. Do you want to keep your eyes here and change how you are using them? Look up, look out, look away. Look ahead, look into, look back. Do you want to go somewhere else and see something different?

Look at what you are looking at and see where you are. See who you are, see what you are a part of, not just to identify yourself, but to look at the world outside yourself and feel the exchange between your small self and this immense, astonishing world.

So often I have looked at the world with the eyes of austerity, the eyes of worry, the eyes of fear. When I was a child visiting New York, my grandfather, a family court justice, took me with him to the court-houses in each of the boroughs and told me stories about the suffering he listened to. As much as I have eyes of compassion, they were a gift from him. Yet my eyes needed to learn to see not only the sorrow in the world but also the wonder. Eyes alert to what's wrong, eager to document the horrors and imbalances, I still see many things that trouble me deeply. But I also honor what is beautiful, whether it is extraordinary, like a

Balinese volcanic mountain terraced with rice fields, or as familiar as the artichokes and raspberries growing in the backyard, or as subtle as the shadows of small stones.

"Beauty surrounds us but sometimes we must be walking in a garden to see it," Rumi declared. Walking in that garden, we observe different things. As we look at the lilac and the plum, the lobelia and the strawberries, the birches and the flower maples, our thoughts can take off and travel on different roads. And at those times when we can't literally be walking in the garden, we can remember the garden in our mind's eye.

There is much to learn about the discipline of feeding the eyes, about celebrating the beauty of the world. I yearn to see through what I know into a truer seeing, not idealizing or diminishing or trying to fit what I see into what I know. Just as we sometimes need to go outside our own personal routines and the garments of our culture to see how they hold us, so we need to extend beyond the usual habits of our vision and our nervous systems to see the rhythms dancing the world into the forms we see. There is a kind of looking that breaks open the distance between the one who looks and that which is looked at. Things look back at us. In certain moments we are received by what we perceive. The more I look at candle flames and white flowers, the light at the edge of the oak trees and the reflection of the sun at dawn, the more I feel the lines of light that connect everything. At those moments, I know that the more we see beauty, the more beauty we are able to see.

The vision that most interests me is both simple and complex. It combines seeing into, seeing through, looking again. Look at a painting or a hillside or a cat or a friend once, and it is all there in that single glance, and then look again until you grow into what you knew in that first seeing.

It is wonderful what we can perceive and create when the eye of imagination and the eye of observation are informed by the eye of love. Photographer Nell Dorr passionately participates in the beauty she experiences by seeing and making pictures. With great intensity she exclaims, "What does bread mean to me—or health, or home, or country or my fellow-man? What does it all mean—Life? Without the one thing, beauty, I think I could not endure to live. With it, I can endure all. I find it equally in joy and in sorrow. In the greatest of each, in birth and in death, I find an almost unbearable beauty . . . [There] is beauty in a calm so deep there is no bottom. There is beauty in silence. There is beauty just in the green world.

"Everyday to waken to it—to feel myself part of it—playing my flute—dancing my part—in tune with the universe—in rhythm with the stars—a camera in my hand. To work itself is holy. The camera cannot see it. You have to see it and not depend too much on exposures. See it. Feel it. Something will come through—a part of it will be there . . . It does not matter what you see, but how. One must come closer. Look deeper . . . To try to share this beauty in pictures is only another way of giving a loaf of bread. The world is being fed with so much fear and horror (along with its wonders) that someone must distribute a simple loaf of bread—and that I feel is my task!"

The ingredients for cultivating our own vision are familiar and close at hand—from listening to our dreams, our senses, our questions, and from looking at what delights us and what we overlook. Perhaps we all work with the same ingredients, but we must each adjust the proportions, must each study the quantities and qualities of the ingredients that make our vision-bread.

We perceive beauty in what we are curious about, what we become connoisseurs of, what we become passionate about and fuss over, what we give ourselves to wholeheartedly. We find beauty in what we love. The Indian poet Ghalib sings, "It's the rose unfolding, that creates the desire to see— / In every color and circumstance, may the eyes be open for what comes." Rumi says, "Borrow the beloved's eyes. See through them and you'll see the beloved everywhere."

According to the Greek philosopher Empedocles, Aphrodite "fashioned our eyes out of the four Greek elements of earth, water, air, and fire, fitting them together with rivets of love. Then, as a man, thinking to make an excursion through the night, prepares a lantern, lighting it at the brightly blazing hearth fire and fitting it around with glass plates to shield it from the winds, so did Aphrodite kindle the fire of the eye at the primal hearth of the universe, confining it with tissues in the sphere of the eye."

Of all the many answers to the question "Who gave you your eyes?" this is the answer that has been the most revealing. Our eyes are a gift from the goddess of beauty; our eyes reflect the beauty of the world.

Kinds of Light, Kind Darkness

Not that the light is holy, but that the holy is the light—
Only by seeing, by being, we know,
Rapt, breath stilled, bliss of the heart.
No microscope nor telescope can discover
The immeasurable: not in the seen but in the seer
Epiphany of the commonplace.
A hyacinth in a glass it was, on my working-table,
Before my eyes opened beyond beauty light's pure living flow.
'It is I,' I knew, 'I am that flower, that light is I,'
'Both seer and sight.'

Kathleen Raine
from "To the Sun"

L ight follows the path of the beautiful," Richard Feynman's high school physics teacher told his easily bored young student. Medieval philosophers perceived the qualities of lucidity and luminosity as attributes of cosmic perfection. Light creates beauty and, often, beauty creates light.

Ancient philosophers believed that it is the light in the eye that sees the light outside. Seeing, then, is as reciprocal as a conversation; we are in fact in a constant conversation with the world we are seeing. Inner light greets outer light—as Goethe wrote, "If the eye were not sunlike, how could we perceive the light?"

When I was researching the subject of night and day for my anthology, *Changing Light*, I read a sentence that struck me. "We can't see light (only its source and its reflection; the light itself is invisible), and we can't see without it." This statement is both obvious and mysterious, a simple physical fact and a wonderful mystical promise. It reminds me of a line from Psalms, "The river of God is full of water." The river of beauty is full of light.

Light, although it is invisible to us, gives us the whole visible world. In everyday life we talk about light as if we see it. It is as if the light we see translates the light we don't see into a language we understand. We turn the light on. We admire the morning light or the mountain light or the way the air is clear and the light is crisp after a rainy day. Sometimes we even talk about the light at the boundaries of the visible spectrum, the "invisible light" of ultraviolet and the infrared.

Scientifically minded people know these marvelous things about light—that each color of light has a different wavelength, that light in a laser is referred to as "coherent light," that infrared looks dark to us because we can't see the light there. Physicists speak of photons; electricians chart wattage; art historians recall the chiaroscuro of the seventeenth century. Physicians remind their clients about seasonal affective disorder. Botanists study the effects of phototropism, mathematicians employ numbers to understand and describe the properties of light. Designers extol the virtues of halogen lamps; carpenters count the number of lights in a window.

Unfamiliar with the terms, I like to hear about foot-candles and the index of refraction and how the light is "incident" upon a surface. Listening to people speak about light, I am reminded that the range of light we can adapt to is incredible, from under a minimum thousandth of a foot-candle to starlight to very bright sunlight. Our eyes adapt in the darkest dark and the brightest light. It takes only a few photons to activate the photoreceptors triggering an electrical impulse to the brain. Although light appears steady, it is actually made of quickly repeated electromagnetic impulses that we perceive as continuous. Light, like our eyes, is always moving. The speed of light in a vacuum is one of the few immutable constants in our ever-changing universe.

As light travels, bumping into things and bouncing off them, it creates shadows and reflections. These words have precise technical definitions, but they also speak to our souls' need for beauty, depth, and balance. In the house where I lived for many years, I mostly remember the afternoon shadows of leaves dancing on the wall in my studio; now it's the morning shadows in the living room that delight me. Shadows of lowered blinds and folding chair, shadows of leaves in the wind, my head and my hand writing. Shadows follow the light, remind us of the movement of light, our changing shapes. I imagine devoting a day to following shadows.

We may not be able to count how many colors we see, or talk about what light is, ultimately. Still we live in relationship to light's rhythms, dance toward it, and perhaps are even made from it. Plants digest light. The whole bodies of primitive invertebrates—coral, jellyfish, sea anemones, starfish—respond to light. Flowers like California poppies and morning glories open and close each day with the sun. Sunflowers move their heads so they are always facing the sun.

As scientists talk about how light is absorbed or scattered, bounced, bent, directed or reflected, I think about what that means in our own lives—how we can absorb light or reflect it, scatter it, long for it. A science book for children declares that anything that radiates light is a light source: "People, plants, and houses do not usually shine but they do reflect light. That is why you see them. Rays of light bounce off them and reach your eyes." Yet, I know people and plants and houses that do shine, lit from within by some mysterious fire. We shine and we burn. Some people are positively incandescent.

For many years, I felt like I wanted to be a cell in the eye of God, though I would sometimes be embarrassed by the sincerity of the image. Now I feel like celebrating that longing. I imagine each being one meets is a part of God's body—even if God does not have a body—and I want to be part of the team of cells whose primary task is to receive and harvest patterns of light, to be one of the cells that inspects and observes the shimmering spirit of all living things, who registers and celebrates color, who studies the patterns of the luminous, the rhythms of light's most amazing music.

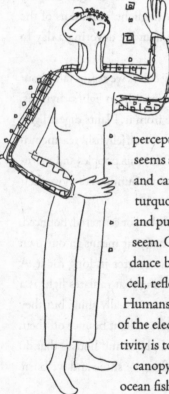

The Alchemy of Color

Colors are not simply pigments and dyes but a form of light, the particular perception of a wavelength. Although color often seems so real that I can taste it, not just in oranges and cantaloupe, blueberries and limes, but also in turquoise glass and indigo jackets, soft gray walls and purple sweaters, colors are not quite what they seem. Color lives not in the things we see but in the dance between object and light, eye cell and brain cell, reflection and absorption, mood and memory. Humans, like most animals, see a very narrow band of the electromagnetic spectrum. Our greatest sensitivity is toward the yellow-green shades of the forest canopy. Bees concentrate on the ultraviolet edge; ocean fish are most alert to blue.

Color is an abstraction, an illusion, far more elusive than we usually acknowledge. The sky blue I have loved for so many years does not live in the sky; the sky is not stained, dyed, or brushed with that blue, although the blue of lakes and oceans mirrors the sky. The blue of the sky comes from our atmosphere deflecting the short "blue" wavelengths of light more effectively than the other colors of the spectrum. In space the sky appears black because there is no atmosphere—no dust or gas—to reflect the light rays from the sun.

The dust of sunset scatters the day's blue, leaving crimson and violet, a blue that is almost pink, a white that hints of blue, a blue that is close to silver, gold, orange, and pale yellow. Appreciation of the sunset is not limited to those with human eyes; chimpanzees, too, like to gather in small groups and watch as the day turns into evening.

I remember walking on a path to the ocean at dusk years ago. And what I'll never find a way to describe: the time of day just past sunset when there is no visible light in the sky. No sun, no moon, no stars. The land shapes seem larger somehow, perhaps because there is no light and shadow. The sky itself is more shaped. The California hills are solid, clear, and definite against the empty, open sky.

The sunset moves us not only because of the beauty of its unpredictable and elusive parade of color. Sunset and the twilight that follows have their own laws and rituals, tones and rhythms, quite apart from the measurement of clock time. It is a time of moments, not minutes, outside the rules of day and night. In its borderland we feel more permeable and vulnerable, open, alert to the silvery questions and shimmering possibilities of our own lives.

"Color is not really necessary for seeing. Motion and contrast would be sufficient," a professor of neuroscience informs me as we sit on the airplane flying out of Denver in the early summer evening. We talk about how a single photon triggers a response in the photoreceptors, the structure of the eagle's eye, the current state of vision research.

Color, then, is a gift. Essential, the way certain gifts become essential, even though we once thought we could survive without them. I learn that until ten million years ago, all flowers were some shade of green, like leaves, and I am in awe of the unnecessary beauty of flowers, the purity of their colors, the most intense colors in nature.

As a child, I often wondered what would happen if we woke up one day and the sky was green and the grass was blue. The capture and imprisonment of the color, leaving us in a black-and-white world, is a common motif in children's stories, a reminder that colors, like music, are deeply connected to the tones and shades of our feelings.

My silver-haired fourth grade teacher, Mrs. Planteen, read to us from a book called *Hailstones and Halibut Bones*, which concluded: "The colors live between black and white in a land that they know best by sight but knowing best isn't everything. Because colors laugh and colors sing, and colors dance and colors cry . . ." She asked us to write poems about colors, drawing my attention to shades and tones, starting an investigation into color that continues to this day.

After I finished my poem about blue, I was so enthusiastic I also wrote about pink and red. I don't remember the poems I wrote, but I do remember the blue cartridge pens staining our fingers as we wrote out our blue headings, blue names, blue dates, and blue subjects, outside the window the blue sky of the Great Plains. Take blue all the way up and it's the white-blue light of summer's dawn, take blue all the way down and we're in the blue-black of winter nights, to the blue-gray of San

Francisco fog, to the blue-violet of Colorado wildflowers, to the blue-green of Oregon forests.

My friend Alice remembers when she was a young woman, working with little kids who were very ill, she overheard a three-year-old with leukemia who had gone in and out of blindness all his life telling another little boy who had never seen at all what the color red was like, his father's red truck. When I tell this story to fifth graders, we try to imagine what red looks like to the hummingbirds, moths, and butterflies. What does red feel like to a little boy who is sometimes blind and to one who has never seen at all?

So many kinds of red. Look at this red poppy, this red rose, this red tile roof, these red shoes, these red words. Moroccan Red, Nebraskan Red, Chinese Red, Mayan Red. I love the way people in New Mexico and Tibet combine turquoise and red. How could you not love purple when red and blue are both so beautiful?

Although I am not a quilter or a weaver, I have mixed up dye baths to dye cloth for batiks, and there was something ancient and powerful and feminine about stirring dye pots and dyeing cloth. I loved the way the cloth turned red immediately, and it took hours for the dark blue dye to set. I love stories of the indigo plant, the Indigo goddess of Africa, the indigo ikat jackets of Japan. I found one at a flea market years ago, dark, dark blue and pale pink, the pink from safflowers. I love the idea of color recipes, cooking up color from all kinds of ingredients, realizing every dye bath is different.

One of my drawing teachers, who had been poisoned by the chemicals in the usual oil paints, returned to the basics, mixing inks from buckeye. Making his own colors became part of his making art. Once he sent us out with an assignment to go into our kitchens and gardens, and try using whatever we found as sources of color—yogurt and turmeric, coffee grounds, flower petals. If I were a weaver, I would experiment with natural dyes, study how the roots of a cherry tree produce a reddish purple, the bark gives tans and oranges, how you make yellow from philodendron and gardenia and red amaryllis flowers. Making color from tree bark and onion skins, mushrooms, marigolds, cranberries, walnut hulls, sassafras roots is a most practical kind of magic.

The ease with which we walk into the art store, the paint store, the fabric store, the makeup counter and find the color we want in tubes and cans and bolts of cloth is relatively recent. Until the nineteenth century, minerals and plants were the main source of color. In the Middle Ages, women used crushed roses and geranium petals to color their lips. Ancient Egyptian women defined their eyes with galena, a type of kohl made from lead ore, and painted their lids with a green unguent made from malachite, which also protected their eyes from the brilliant sun. They stained their lips with a red-ochre pigment combined with oil.

The Egyptians valued making pigments as an art that preceded and rivaled alchemy. In China, painting and alchemy were both regarded as transformative arts. Alchemy was the "art of yellow and white," a reference to gold and silver; painting was called the art of "red and blue," from cinnabar and azurite. Gold and silver were the colors of immortality, cinnabar and azurite the colors of life.

In India, color is emotional and symbolic. An Indian text names five different kinds of white: bright golden white, ivory white, pure sandal white, autumn cloud white, and autumn moon white, and I think of an elementary school student who also named kinds of white—egg white and clay white, cloud white and paper white, diamond white, mayonnaise white, mushroom white. I remember a morning I spent reading to Alzheimer's patients, and how one of the men said, "Color is a language we don't have to teach our brain to understand," and together we composed a poem:

Color is a language
we don't have to teach our brain to understand.
Color explains itself.
Red is there.
Green is right there next to it.
Each speaks its own language.
We don't tell them what they are.
They tell us what they are.

"Colors are feelings, you just can't see them," a third grader writes. "Orange shares colors with yellow and red," is how a second grader describes color mixing. "Orange loves the poppy," another third grader proclaims. In *Children's Letters to God*, a child writes, "Dear God, I didn't think that orange went with purple until I saw the sunset you made last night."

Growing up, there seemed to be a lot of rules about what colors "matched" or "clashed" that didn't make sense. Why did blue and purple go together if red and purple didn't? A friend told me, to her mother's horror, she liked to wear pink and orange! I think of the house around the corner with the poppies, red and orange and magenta, all mixed together, that are such a joy to walk past.

Some of us clothe our ideas in colors, need color to think. In *Wisdom and the Senses*, Joan Erikson,

41

the wife of psychologist Erik Erikson, describes how she set up the warp of her loom to illustrate her husband's theory of development. "The threads themselves had duplicated the black-and-white chart—but in color. For the first time my mind and my senses collaborated and made the idea manifest. I understood; I knew. Moreover, those empty boxes of black-and-white chart were now literally full of meaning. What does the blue of trust do to the orange of autonomy, coupled with the gray of shame and doubt? I see supporting blue lines of hope in the second lower-left-hand square. In the top line of the final weaving, observe how all the early strengths present themselves, bolstering the purple stage of aging."

"Color is contagious," the artist whose workshop I'm in says, as I find myself mixing purple and brown like my neighbor at the easel next to mine. Her shapes are organic, woven in and out of each other; mine geometric, separate except for this wonderful silver that I dip my hands into and apply around the edges of the purple. I walk out of the studio, and a few hours later I am sitting in a Vietnamese restaurant eating eggplant *satay* in a gray-green room full of bright red paper lanterns. I had spent the afternoon painting a deep turquoise face and not remembering how a nose looks. I look at my friend's face like I have never seen a face before. The angles of his face, the geometry, the landscapes are like a book, only the text is inside out. Maybe the shapes I make on the page are only an excuse to look at things more carefully, to let my eyes touch the world with more curiosity and care. I reach for colors because there are no words for the "everythingness" and the "all of this-ness." I reach for colors because I don't know how to sing.

Looking and looking (except looking only begins to describe it), it's like studying and tasting and almost like hearing, it's eager and hungry and patient and urgent. There are so many layers in the emotional geography of one face. Sometimes the world is so full of color it is almost unbearable.

Color gives me my eyes. Colors become like qualities, like characters, like places we can travel toward and return from. Colors are like companions; when we start to take them for granted, they startle us with their beauty. I meet certain people in the territory of turquoise, others in the purple lands, others in the state of indigo. My sister and I meet in light aqua and violet. My friend Marian and I meet in pale pink with her daughters close by. Marty and I meet in silver-green, sometimes called sage, and the deep turquoise known as teal.

Colors live different lives at night than they do during the day. At night the dark colors are less intense, and the pastels that seemed meek and agreeable during the day take on more authority. Pale pink is lovely during the day but at night her charm becomes more regal. Silver gray, introverted, curious, articulate during the day, comes alive in a whole other way at night. Indigo, my favorite collaborator, can stay up all night if necessary. Dark green likes to stay inside during the winter months, curled up under the comforter, snuggled up close with her sewing, telling stories to her loved ones.

The colors meet to discuss and plan our seasons, rotate the assignments so one year Purple and Bright Green and Yellow are waiting for Dr. Gray to go on vacation so they can bring out the spring, the next year Gray is part of the planning committee that includes Fuchsia and Mustard and Sage.

Colors, like hemlines and haircuts and car shapes, go in and out of style, becoming popular partly through sharp marketing, partly through the movement of the collective mind. We hunger for the audacity of red, yearn for the elegance of black, request the comfort of deep green, thirst for the serenity of pale blue, need more tenderness in our lives and find it not only in pale peach but also in deep brown.

When we wear certain colors, it is as if we are entering their territory, their jurisdictions. A friend explains, and I have to agree, that on certain days one needs a particular color. The next day that same color is irritating, almost itchy. We clothe ourselves in color, wrap colors around us for protection and inspiration, for clarity and warmth. We wear a color and then the color wears us. I like to wear solid colors, tones of deep green and pale green, tones of burnt orange and peach and pink, shades of blue and purple. I love the flat blocks of color in Byzantine icons and Russian abstract painting, indigo circles and orange squares, green spirals and purple triangles. I often think of color as substantial and solid; I have to pinch myself to remember that color is fluid and moving, shaped by light, renewed by light, and itself, always, a form of light.

The Feminine Face of Light

I am trying to remember when I first heard about the goddess. Was it a mention of Marilyn Monroe as a sex goddess in a *Time* magazine article I read in sixth grade or the image of Venus de Milo painted on a truck as a logo for a neighborhood dry cleaning business? As a girl I loved learning about the ancient world, and I remember being curious about the Babylonian idol worshippers referred to in our religious school texts, not learning until much later that those idols were often goddesses. In junior high I prepared an elaborate report about the gods and goddesses of early Egypt, and as part of my research I went downtown to the beautiful museum with the marble walls and gazed into the cases filled with blue-beaded necklaces and ancient earrings. These experiences gave me the impression that goddesses were from distant civilizations—or Hollywood. The real power was God, and although ultimately beyond gender, God was always identified as "He."

Sometimes I imagine an apartment building where all the gods and goddesses live. And then there is a whole other place where God lives, beyond any of our names for Source, beyond all the aspects and myths and stories and names, so much bigger and wider and brighter than anything we can say in words. Yet, I am immensely nourished by the "Return of the Goddess," the renaissance of women's spirituality in the last thirty years. Working with the Divine as Mother, hearing God spoken of as "Her," addressed as "She," has opened up new ways for us to see women, to reach and stretch and lean and bend toward God. To address God as Mother is to offer us possibilities of wholeness that we have long been denied. Too often we are told to choose between power and love, beauty and intelligence, strength and wisdom.

To call out to the female God, God as Bride and Grandmother, Changing Woman, is to embrace this world we have so often denied in the name of a transcendent God, to begin to heal our isolation and estrangement. The world of the Goddess is the world of here and now. Much of the beauty of the ancient goddesses comes from their embodiment of the sacred and the sexual, their appreciation of all expressions of life energy.

Although we usually associate the sun with male gods, and the moon is identified as female, sun goddesses are coming to light as contemporary feminist scholars untangle the omissions, assumptions, and distortions of earlier researchers. Sun goddesses are found in Australia and the Amazon, but also in Lithuania and Korea, Finland and Egypt, among the Cherokee and native peoples of central California. Sun goddesses maintain the earth through their weaving and spinning, count out the rhythms of light and dark, life and death. Stories of the sun goddesses give us images of the soul's journey to wholeness.

When Amaterasu, the Japanese sun goddess, could no longer endure her brother's cruel treatment of her weaving women, she retreated into a mountain cave, and the world was plunged into a cold, dark gloom. Eight hundred deities gathered in front of the cave, begging her to return. Their music and song was heard throughout the world, but she stayed inside. Finally, aware that Amaterasu had never seen herself, they mounted a large octagonal mirror near the entrance. An elderly goddess began a wild, erotic dance. Hearing the cheers and cries of the others, Amaterasu was overcome with curiosity. She slid back the boulder, and her brightness threw off a dazzling reflection. Attracted to this unknown radiance, she cautiously moved toward it, and one of the gods quickly blocked the cave entrance. When Amaterasu returned, the light was restored, and it continues to bless us to this day.

About ten years ago, I dreamt I was showing a man where the ruins of Aphrodite were buried in the middle of a downtown Midwestern city. He noted that she is almost forgotten, except for the occasional places named after her like restaurants and hair salons, massage parlors and dry cleaners.

Aphrodite is golden, laughter-loving, reminding us that passion in relationship, in art, in life, brings light and delight. She is a goddess of the dawn and of the seas, goddess of love and beauty, goddess of ecstasy and radiance. She is identified with many kinds of birds, with dolphins, with the life-sustaining rain, with the natural rhythms of the seasons, with fertility and ripening, with roses and lilies and apples. Animals are attracted to her, the gray wolves and grim-eyed lions, the bears and swift leopards. Passionate and powerful, Aphrodite is a goddess of nature and culture.

In a society dominated by greed and frightened of love, we forget the freedom and generosity of Aphrodite's sensual nature, her light, her charms. We miss Aphrodite more than we know; we need her to know our own aliveness. Her purest instinct is to embody and to appreciate grace and beauty. She brings a sweetness that renews our hearts. In a very real way we share her exile. In "All the Spring Lends Itself to Her," the poet Linda Gregg begins:

> *If Her skirt does not bend the grass, nor sea air*
> *mold Her shape while She is happy, there is no grace.*
> *I will not stop looking for that. Song and color*
> *circle in the air for Her to stand in.*

Gregg tells us, "She is not needed for this world to be a success / Either way the other powers will have their time." And concludes with a note of yearning:

> *If love does not reign,*
> *we are unsuited for the season of ripeness.*
> *If we do not see Her body in the glass of this beauty,*
> *the sun will blind us. We will lie in the humming fields*
> *and call to Her, coaxing Her back. We will lie*
> *pressed close to the earth, calling Her name,*
> *wondering if it is Her voice we are whispering.*

As Aphrodite has become a refugee, we have been left with a simultaneous distrust and hunger for pleasure, sensuality, creativity. A dancer recalls showing a young girl the sunset coming through lace curtains and the girl responding, "Now I understand why you dance." We are stirred by Her beauty, the beauty of our world, moved to offer our most gracious response.

To speak of the Goddess is to offer women a mirror in which we, like Amaterasu, can glimpse our own radiance. The Goddess becomes another name for our longing to be whole and our wholeness, our audacity and our subtlety, our longing for gentleness, our need for beauty.

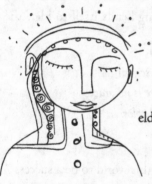

Radiance

"We need more light as we grow older," says Linda Sanford, who designs lighting for the elderly. "We need more time to adapt from light to dark. By the time we're in our forties, it is noticeable. By sixty, we need two or three times as much light."

We need more light as we grow older. An absolute physical fact, yes, but also a metaphor for our increasing need for spiritual nourishment. Our lives begin in darkness, the shelter of the womb. Our days begin in darkness. We emerge from the darkness, return to it briefly each night. We live in darkness and dim light and bright light.

Our ancestors, knowing how utterly dependent they were on the light of the sun, expressed their gratitude for light in daily prayers and seasonal rituals. Throughout the world people honored the solstices and equinoxes, lit candles to mark transitions into night, into holy time.

Religious texts from ancient India, the writings of medieval Jewish mystics, Japanese poems praising the moon are drenched with light. Angels and saints are outlined with gold, shining with devotion, etched with light. Discovering the candlelit churches of Assisi when I was nineteen, my friends and I walked outside the basilica at twilight and felt how the light continued, accompanying us as we walked on ancient streets in the cold November hills. Where did all this radiance come from?

What would the world be like if we were more curious about light and less afraid to admit our own luminosity? How would our sense of beauty expand if we actively inspired each other to bring forward the light we each carry?

There are many ways to experience light, and the eyes may not be as necessary as we think. The person whose writing about light has most moved me was a Frenchman who went blind at the age of eight. Jacques Lusseyran organized a student resistance group during the Nazi occupation of Paris and was one of the few French inmates to survive Buchenwald. His memoir *And There Was Light* shines likes a chandelier full of candles in a dark house on a long winter's night.

Throughout his life, Lusseyran had an extraordinarily vivid relationship to light. He recalls the light in his childhood as if it were a playmate. "I was always running; the whole of my childhood was spent running. Only I was not running to catch hold of something. That is a notion for grownups and not the notion of a child. I was running to meet everything that was visible, and everything I could not yet see . . ." He evokes the sensations of chasing light. "I was just about to jump into it, with my feet together, at the end of the path; to catch hold of it as you catch a butterfly over the pond; to lie down with it in the grass or on the sand. Nothing else in nature, not even the sounds to which I listened so attentively, was as precious to me as light."

In the spring of his eighth year, Lusseyran was blinded after a fall. The curiosity and courage with which he meets and explores his blindness is as inspiring as anything I've ever read. "I began to look more closely, not at things but at a world closer to myself, looking from an inner place to one further within, instead of clinging to the movement of sight toward the world outside." He experiments with this light, observing how the light fades with fear, jealousy, and anger. He notices the way people take on certain colors—a girl he is drawn to is bright and red with red shadows. He describes living in a stream of light: "I was not light myself, I knew that, but I bathed in it as an element which blindness had suddenly brought much closer. I could feel light rising, spreading, resting on objects, giving them form, then leaving them."

Lusseyran invites us to acknowledge an inner vision that is rarely described, to deepen our fields of awareness. His dedication to the inner light of attention is a beautiful teaching about focusing on the essential. Because he speaks so simply, eloquently, and unpretentiously, his celebration of light is compelling and profound, the radiance of his truth burning away the illusions that constitute true blindness.

❧

In creation stories across the Americas, Europe, Asia, Africa, light breaks open the world. Sometimes the light is God's great gift, and sometimes Mink steals the sun, Coyote spills the stars, Prometheus takes the fire. In many stories it is through an act of cunning, trickery, theft, that light is brought to the world.

In the Northwest creation myth, Raven notices that only one man in the world has all the light. He keeps it to himself trapped within many nested boxes, afraid to see if his daughter is as ugly as a sea creature or as beautiful as hemlock fronds at sunrise. Raven arranges to be born to the old man's daughter. As a young boy he charms his grandfather, gaining his confidence and affection. When he first attempts to hold the box of light, the grandfather is very angry. Over time, Raven successfully demands to play with the progressively smaller boxes that contain the light. Finally, after many days of cajoling and tantrums, the grandfather allows his grandson to hold the light for a moment.

Instantly, Raven changes back into himself and flies away, intending, like the old man, to keep the golden ball of light for himself. However, he is having such a good time flying with the light that he doesn't see Eagle until he approaches. Raven swerves to avoid Eagle's claws, dropping much of the light, which breaks into pieces and bounces back into the sky to become the moon and the stars. Eagle follows Raven out beyond the rim of the world. Finally, exhausted by the long chase, Raven relinquishes the last piece of light, and it becomes the sun. As the sun's rays reach the old man, who has been weeping in his house bitterly disappointed by his grandson's treachery and theft, he sees his daughter for the first time, beautiful as the fronds of the hemlock tree in the early spring morning.

As we let in more light, vision becomes clearer, the heart lightens, music is more beautiful. Those, like the grandfather, who try to keep light to themselves, are lost in a darkness that conceals the beauty they so much want to see. We glorify the light, romanticize darkness, yet all too often stay ignorant of both. Light helps us understand darkness, just as darkness teaches us about light. Sometimes we hide our light, pretending to be less than we are, hiding our inner knowing behind comfortable stories we haven't taken the time to question. It's not our light to hide; it's not our light to hoard. Our light does not belong to us, even though we are responsible for it.

We need to distinguish between the tired-out darkness in which fear and anger dominate and keep us apart and the darkness that Lusseyran describes as light at a slower rate, the jeweled darkness that ends each day. The darkness that I value is the darkness of the vast night sky illuminated by stars. It is the darkness of immense possibilities, the sweet dark wisdom of night, a darkness that isn't only black but the deepest blues, the richest purples, the most intense browns. It includes the darkness of conception and gestation, the darkness of rich soil, the darkness of great distances and the darkness that dissolves all distance.

I love the light that comes in through our eyes and the light that goes out from the eyes of those I love. Sometimes inside one human being there is so much space, glimpsing inside takes one deep into an ocean. The eye like a star reflected in the night-sky waters. Light dances through water, at the edges of clouds.

When the light breaks up and breaks through the darkness, we are shown what needs our attention. It is as if light is always teaching us, giving us new assignments, revealing what needs to be purified, transformed, sanctified. Light is a language as necessary as touch, as essential as beauty. Light penetrates and hides inside places we never expect to find it. Light enters through the cracks in the windows, through curtains and shut eyes. Jacques Lusseyran encourages us to study light, to seek and to see, to be alive to the ever-changing light, to go deeper and deeper into the darkness and still find light. To go forward when one is afraid and find courage in the midst of the fears, courage to face what is awful and what is awesome, courage to face the shadows that light creates. At the end of *And There Was Light* Lusseyran writes, "Joy does not come from outside, for whatever happens to us it is within . . . light does not come to us from without. Light is in us, even if we have no eyes."

Light illuminates the world around us, articulating what we see but cannot say. In *Catching the Light*, the physicist Arthur Zajonc notes:

"Novalis wrote wisely when he said that with the flame, all natural forces are active. The truth of his words rests on the fact that the flame, and the light it sheds, are as much moral and spiritual forces as natural ones. Light is not two things, but one. Its efficacy lies in the unity. The scientific study of light never need diminish its full stature. But we, like Navajo gods, walk a fragmented landscape riven by canyons and gorges. Unlike them, we are timid, holding fast to the firm familiar soil beneath our feet, unwilling to throw a rainbow bridge across the dark chasms of the world. Not lunacy, but courage is needed to see our world whole, to know that love must become concentric with insight."

We are little bits of light, yearning to be lighter. Each of us carries a small piece of the light. We need to stand next to each other, like trees do. Standing beside each other, we begin to make enough light to see, to see our way together.

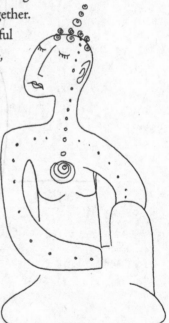

Light is the most mysterious and beautiful fact of all, belonging to no one and everyone, living in Thoreau's notebook where poetry and science are impossible to distinguish. The inner firelight of the great seers and seekers is of the same stuff that lights up the night sky with distant starfire. The poet and naturalist John Daniel writes: "What I call mine, what I call mind, is a light I borrow from the light of the sky. And as the change comes to sky and field, the last shadows blending into dusk, the clarity of things dissolving, darkness composing itself, the only light left is that glowing within."

Mirrors & Windows

Everyone wants to fall in love in a strange town,
Everyone wants to dive in that river of dreams
where the incense swirls toward the stars
and the mirrors on the hearts of the saints
make it impossible to lie to yourself.

John Oliver Simon
from "Gringo Trail"

I dream that I am in a forest where all the trees have mirrors hanging from their branches. Walking through these trees, there are so many reflections of sky and green leaf and branch and sunlight, it is impossible to keep track of all the trees. In the dream I hear a line from a poem, "Is the one I love everywhere?" I remember one of my favorite questions: What is the difference between a mirror and a window? We look in the mirror to see ourselves. We look out the window to see the world. Taking our cue from mirrors, which turn things around and reverse them, perhaps we can look in the mirror and see the world, look out the window and find ourselves.

Technically, the difference between the window and the mirror is that the window transmits light, the mirror reflects light. We can make a fire with a mirror. Water is one of my favorite mirrors. In science experiments, mirrors become tools to learn about the directions and qualities of light. Extending our vision, bringing the distant closer, mirrors reflect and reveal the nature of the universe. Mirrors can also be used as tools to learn about ourselves. Narcissism, literally, or self-awareness. Self-judgment or appreciation. Mirrors have many purposes, uses, mysteries; they always involve light, ignite vision, offer insight.

Our eyes are mirrors and windows, reflecting, collecting, and transmitting light. We are mirrors, revealing ourselves to each other with attention and interest; we are windows that open into the strange landscapes of each other's familiar worlds. We look out from behind the windows of our eyes. And the light inside meets and greets the light outside. Mirror and window becomes another way of talking about insight and outlook, the double nature of seeing.

Mirrors: Reflecting Identity, Revealing Soul

Mirror, derived from the Latin "to look at, to wonder at," is cousin to *admire* and *smile*, *mirage* and *miracle*. *Mirabella*: strange, wonderful beauty. Mirrors bring us into mythlands, moonlands, mystery lands. Lakes are mirrors, metaphor is a mirror, poetry is a two-way mirror. The Persian poets called the moon "the mirror of time." Oliver Wendell Holmes called photography "the mirror with a memory." In restaurants and dance studios, in dressing rooms and bars, in French cafés, on the walls of European palaces, sewn on the coats of Siberian shamans, mirrors report back to us who we are, offer a large or small reflection, a shiny fragment, a segment, a watery glimpse.

Metaphoric associations with mirrors are numerous and contradictory, emphasizing both vanity and awareness. Mirrors are mentioned in the titles of murder mysteries and memoirs, as well as Web sites, Buddhist texts, literary studies. The mirrors multiply the images, expand the space in the room, bounce light around. In the Chinese practice of feng shui, mirrors are used both to bring things toward us and to push things away. Fantasy writers, poets, and filmmakers have long seen mirrors as doorways that open both to parts of ourselves and to other worlds.

All over the world, people have believed that mirrors both reflect and capture the soul. Mirrors offer protection; mirrors are dangerous. Narcissus fell in love with his own reflection in the pond. For centuries, throughout the "mirror belt" from Iran through Afghanistan, Pakistan, and across India, small mirrors have been embroidered on garments and horse gear to form mosaic patterns. Linked to solar worship and water, these shiny talismanic mirrors are both protective and decorative; they offer back small, dazzling glimpses of sunlight.

There's something mysterious about our mirror images, like our shadows, like photographs—as if a part of us lives in that two-dimensional alias. Ancient Egyptians and Chinese buried their dead with mirrors, believing that they were a necessary tool for the soul's journey into the next world. Eastern Europeans and Orthodox Jews cover the mirrors in their houses as part of the process of mourning, concentrating the attention inward, away from the distractions of earthly life. To Haitians, mirrors signify the watery domain of the deities, where souls reside for a year after dying. Tibetans wear silver mirrors around their necks. There is an East Indian folk custom that a bride is supposed to look at her husband for the first time through her mirrored ring.

Throughout its history, the mirror has been used both as a practical object and as a conduit to the eternal. Thousands of years ago, our ancestors polished special stones to make "natural" mirrors, looked at themselves in lakes and rivers. Later, they used shiny pieces of metal, including copper and bronze, obsidian, pyrite, silver. The first known mirror, from Catal Huyuk in what is now Turkey, dates back to 6,000 BC Early

Egyptian mirrors were selenium and slate that needed to be wet to give back a reflection. Later Egyptian mirrors were made from copper, bronze, and silver, shaped like the sun at the horizon. The Egyptian mirror, used for applying cosmetics and for rituals of adornment and spiritual consecration, became the prototype for mirrors around the ancient world.

In Roman times, bronze mirrors were so common that servants had mirrors; in the Middle Ages, mirrors had become so rare that they were often exchanged as gifts between kings and queens. By the time of the Renaissance, Venice had become famous for its high-quality mirrors. The Venetian glassmakers had discovered the art of taking clear, colorless glass and backing it with a bright silvery amalgam of tin and mercury. The seventeenth-century Venetian mirror makers maintained a highly profitable monopoly as they exported mirror glass to European cities, the Islamic world, and India.

By the time the Sun King, Louis XIV, reached the throne, the French were spending a fortune on Venetian mirrors, embellishing the boudoirs and dressing rooms of ordinary citizens and the state rooms of the king. Colbert, the king's adviser, lured a succession of Venetian craftsmen to court with lucrative pensions, but the Venetians took steps to bring the renegade craftsmen home. The drama continued over a period of several years, and two men died in mysterious circumstances that suggested poisoning before the French succeeded in unlocking the secrets and mastering the craft.

Within the century, mirror-making was practiced extensively throughout Europe, especially in Paris and London. The clarity and size of looking glasses continued to improve as mirrors became part of the interior decor of the home. Large wall mirrors over the fireplace were lit by the nearby candlesticks. Mirrors decorated wardrobes and women's vanities.

We commonly associate mirrors with the world of appearances, interior decorating, the decoration of self, illusion and vanity. However, mirrors also tell us about the journey to self-knowledge, to increasingly accurate perception, true insight. Among the ancient Hittites of Turkey, in Korea and Siberia, India and Ireland, mirrors were sacred artifacts used in sun ceremonies and rituals, reflecting reverence for the sun's great light. Mirrors were placed on the altars of the ancient goddess, and the handles of Egyptian metal mirrors were often made to represent the body of the goddess Hathor so that the viewer's face appears in the circle above the goddess's body.

Chinese and Tibetan Buddhists have developed rituals to cleanse, purify, and illuminate the mind by cleaning a mirror in which the image of Buddha is reflected. The Chinese mirror was a tangible metaphor for wisdom; the mirror received the light and reflected the truth. Early Chinese mirrors were highly valued talismans, revered as a symbol of the universe, given as gifts on special holidays, weddings, and state occasions. Round mirrors suggested the canopy of heaven. The backs of mirrors were inscribed with emblems for the directions and the animals of the Chinese zodiac. Bronze marriage mirrors, symbolizing fidelity, were decorated with pairs of animals, sparrows and butterflies. I've heard that the mirrors in women's makeup compacts are related to sacred mirrors of ancient China, and I like the way this brings together the cosmic and the cosmetic.

On a personal level, mirrors speak of identity

and appearance; they instruct us about the changing face of time, the journey between self-criticism and appreciation, the interplay between looks and character, the changing and unchanging face of the soul. What do you see when you look in the mirror? What is your intention: to scrutinize, to criticize, to polish, to appreciate? Mirrors focus energy; they offer us the opportunity to look at how we use their focus. For a moment it's useful to look *at* the mirror instead of *into* the mirror.

My neighbor took down the large wall mirrors that were in her bathroom and replaced them with hand mirrors of various sizes and shapes—oval, round, square, even the polished reflective surface of a retired hard drive. She reports that she was tired of confronting herself full on in the big mirrors, but she enjoys seeing a little of herself at a time. Her wall of mirrors reminds us of the purpose of the bathroom as the place in which we go about our preparations to become visible, arranging our appearance before facing outward.

Thirty-five years ago, anthropologist Edmund Carpenter described the reaction of Biami Highlanders when they first encountered their reflections in large mirrors. Although a few men had scraps of mirror about the size of coins, Carpenter didn't see any surfaces for reflection in the countryside or the village, and he doubted that the Biami had ever seen themselves: "Certainly their initial reaction to the large mirrors suggested this was a new experience for them. They were paralyzed. After their first startled response—covering their mouths and ducking their heads—they stood transfixed, staring at their images, only their stomach muscles betraying great tension. In a matter of days, however, they groomed themselves openly before mirrors."

I don't know if the presence of more mirrors in our lives has given us any more knowledge of ourselves. Perhaps it has simply made us more self-conscious and self-critical. We have so many opinions about our appearance, and yet we don't know what we truly look like. We hardly see ourselves, but we have all kinds of ideas about how others see us. The woman who cuts my hair stands all day in a roomful of mirrors. Emily notices what people will say to her face in the mirror and what they will turn to her and say when they face her. As she observes the difference between what we see when we look in the mirror and what others see when they look at us, and hears the way we attack our looks, she imagines inventing a little magical mirror we could wear on top of our heads that would show others how we see ourselves.

In her installation *Mirror, Mirror*, Bay Area artist Lorraine Weglarz reconstructs a women's dressing room. Across the mirror in red lipstick she writes a sampling of the negative comments we use to greet our reflections. Weglarz challenges the viewer to witness herself surrounded by the angry words scribbled across the mirror. Whether the messages come from the self or a person who criticized us or the culture, all three throw off their energies in the three-way mirror. Weglarz exposes a layer of hate and aggression that usually is private, hidden, shameful. As we unmask and witness the mantras of complaint and hear the language in which we run ourselves down, we observe the amount of energy lost to this disease of self-hate. We begin to develop compassion for the ways we judge ourselves.

"Growing up, I felt like a ghost. I needed to look in the mirror to know I was real," a woman notes. The hunger in her statement is haunting; it is a reminder of how lonely we are, how we want not only to be reflected, but to be loved and cherished. A man reports that because his parents could not mirror him he went to the window, and he continued to look out into the larger world to locate himself until he learned he could also look inside.

A boutique owner confides that she decided not to place mirrors in the dressing rooms because her women customers typically focus on critiquing their body shapes before they see the clothes. She prefers that they come out in the open where she can add her feedback to the mirror's reflection. In a very gentle, matter-of-fact way, she is acknowledging the harsh way we look at ourselves, and the gift we give by seeing each other more objectively.

A friend describes visiting a church in southern Mexico where all the statues of the saints in the church are adorned with mirrors. "The thing about the mirrors," she says, "is that as you come through, pass by the statues of the saints, you look in the mirror and see your own face. Looking at your face, that's how you decide if you need to confess anything." Or as the poet John Oliver Simon writes, "The mirrors on the hearts of saints make it impossible to lie to yourself."

Our faces change the more we look at them, into our familiar features. It is a challenge to be able to look in the mirror until we see ourselves, a challenge to continue to look in the mirror until we stop seeing ourselves and see only a human face. If we can look at our own faces respectfully and honestly, we can begin to see each other.

The Mirror of Relationship

Hiking on a clear day in Colorado, I am stunned to see how the creek mirrors clouds. Walking at the ocean I love the way the ocean mirrors the sky. Always this companionship between earth and sky. Waters of the earth stand as mirrors to the sun.

One of my favorite dictionary definitions describes a mirror as "anything that faithfully reflects or gives a true picture of something else." Like the clouds becoming visible in the creek with certain angles of light, we are mirrors for each other. Water mirrors water. Light meets light. We yearn to be seen; we are eager to be mirrored, reflected, understood. We begin to know each other by seeing each other's faces—moods and features, we are drawn in and withdraw. Vibrant and vulnerable, sour and tender, in the faces of others we meet ourselves, aspects and expressions that scare us and delight us. As mirrors, we offer each other multiple impressions. I look at you to discover you and to discover myself, to rediscover you and rediscover myself.

The word *pupil* is derived from the Latin for "doll" or "little girl," referring to the tiny reflection of oneself mirrored back when looking very closely at another's eyes.

The Germans refer to the little man in the pupil, the Spanish to *el niño del ojo*. We meet ourselves in the eyes of friends, children, lovers, strangers.

Sometimes the best way to be seen is to start to see, to become the

mirror. Who is it easy to be a mirror for? Who is it difficult to mirror? In the dance of similars and opposites, how do we mirror our intimates? What do we offer them? We learn again and again that we can't change or control a lover, a child, a parent, a best friend, a spouse. We have no control, and yet we can offer a loving reflection.

Sometimes the mirror breaks. Illusions shatter. And we find out we don't need to be mirrored in the same way. What kind of relationship is possible when we no longer need the other to affirm our reality?

I imagine human beings are like vessels filled with water. Partially acquainted with the vessel, partially acquainted with the water. Inside the vase, we spill out, we overflow and leak; we swim around half blind, often unaware of how we are moving in space, ignorant of our true faces and forms. We discover faces we didn't even know we had when we meet our face in another. We learn not only how we appear but what we are capable of through bumping up against each other, meeting in his face, seeing in her eyes, our terror, our beauty, ugliness, fear, and love. Perceived, received, the soul's feelings and thoughts are partially revealed in our outer forms. We lose and find each other, lose and find ourselves.

Some friends offer the mirror as a gift; some carry the mirror in anger. Some companions bring the mirror reluctantly, others willingly. Sometimes we need a mirror held up to illuminate our illusions. A teacher hands you the mirror and sends you home to look at yourself; another becomes the mirror and insists that you stand where you are and see what you are doing. Mierle Laderman Ukeles, the artist in residence at the New York City Department of Sanitation for more than twenty years, once mounted mirrors on the side of a garbage truck, calling it *The Social Mirror*. Her vehicle became a mirror to awareness, to what we discard, a window into the way we treat those who collect our trash.

I remember being six and going to a friend's house for lunch, looking at her as she appeared in the mirror of her mom's horizontal bureau. As

I looked at her in the looking glass, I experienced an intense curiosity to be behind her eyes and see the world the way it looked to her.

Although I didn't have the language at the time, my curiosity was accompanied by great tenderness. I thought, *She has a different life than me. She lives in different rooms. She hangs her clothes in the closet, and we fold ours in drawers. Her mother cuts the sandwiches in four triangles instead of squares. When she walks to school, she walks on different streets. The world looks different to her.* This experience repeats itself from time to time. It is an act of both empathy and creativity to imagine what the world looks like from someone else's eyes.

We expect to find the world outside the window, expect to find ourselves in the mirror. But I am interested in what happens when we let the world be our mirror, go deeper into ourselves and find the world, go out into the world and find ourselves anew. The Kogi Indians of Colombia describe this reciprocity by saying: "We always make offerings to the sun and to the mountains and to the stars. That is why we live here." A young girl writes, "I didn't know there was another me in the world. It seems like every time I smell a flower I see myself."

The Huichol of northern Mexico regard being beautiful as an act of devotion. Their traditional clothes enfold them in the beauty of the natural world. The embroidered flower ponchos and white pants stitched with bright colorful vines, intricately beaded earrings, necklaces, bracelets are alive with the abundance and color of the earth. Because the Huichol see themselves as mirrors of the sacred, they regard their colorful and ornate clothing as a source of pleasure to their gods and goddesses.

"The world is no more than the Beloved's single face. In the desire of the one to know its own beauty we exist," the poet Ghalib exclaims. We are not alone. The world we face faces us. We look out and the world looks back at us.

Windows to Beauty

The mirror becomes a window: we are mirrors for each other, and suddenly we discover that we are also windows, each of us, into worlds we couldn't know without each other. New views break into our lives, our minds. "He was the window that introduced me to the language of the wind." "She was the window that taught me to listen to the language of travelers and messengers, the world of air currents and the life cycle of cloudy things." During a time of crisis, a friend visiting from out of town washes my cloudy studio windows, and the room is suddenly bright; I'm touched by the practicality and simplicity of her gift.

As much as we hunger to be reflected, to be mirrored, we also need the opening into a larger world that many windows present. Windows, transparent doors, open wide and close tight, bring light and air into the room, the sounds of children playing at the school three blocks away, the smell of the neighbor's barbecue. Windows interrupt the life inside with messages, secret songs, wind stories.

There are representations of windows in early wall paintings from Egypt and bas reliefs from Assyria; the small openings in house walls were covered with matting. I love the windows in old houses, the doors with many panes, the subdivided sections called "lights." The round stained-glass windows of European cathedrals offer spiritual instruction as well as immense beauty. The way light comes through tall windows in certain simple churches is breathtaking, windows to eternity.

What draws you to your favorite window? Is it the view out it offers, the light that comes in and fills the room? Is it the comfort of curling up in a window seat and daydreaming? An intimate view into a neighbor's yard or an expansive view of lights across a valley? The windows sit at the edges between the house and garden, between the intimacy of a room and the immensity of the world. Windows rest, like our eyes, at the intersection between the light inside and the light outside. What is your favorite window becomes a question not just of what landscape or cityscape you like to look at; it is also a question of how much nourishment you take in from the earth, how much from the sky.

I recently visited friends in the mountains, a writer and a sculptor, who have a cozy house and a large, wonderful studio. One long wall of the studio is filled with three rows of windows, acknowledging the mineral, plant, and sky views. Windows, large and small, horizontal and vertical, frame rock and tree branch, hillside and New Mexico sky. It is delightful to be inside looking at all the different vignettes and views and then go outside and see the whole uninterrupted landscape. Like my neighbor's bathroom wall decorated with all the small mirrors, each window frames a piece of the whole.

I had thought a window was a door for the wind, but etymologically, a window is a compound of *wind* and *eye*, an eyelike opening for the air. When I first lived on Diamond Street in San Francisco, I'd cross Market Street and climb a steep hill to a small park that looked out on the city. From my hill, there was a wonderful view of the idiosyncratic houses growing up and down the hills and valleys. And all the windows in the houses did seem like eyes, looking back at you, hundreds of eyes, letting in light, curtained and shuttered and closed up at night.

The warm yellow light coming out of certain living room windows in the evening has always been beautiful to me. Recently, on a night walk a friend and I tromped down the wooden path among Sausalito houseboats, and it was wonderful to see the rectangular light from the windows reflected in the water as calligraphic dashes of light in the waves.

The second-story windows at the yoga studio face west toward the bay. Through the year we watch the light, from solstice to equinox to solstice; as our practice deepens, the days grow longer, then shorter, and we are again practicing in the dark. The changing light becomes a companion to our practice.

I spend a lot more time looking out windows than looking in mirrors. Windows are essential to my sanity. When I'm inside, I almost always want to be at the window. For me, to look out and up is not a distracting but a deepening, a remembering. I need to be near a window when I work. In my last office I looked out on a big palm tree; now I see my neighbor's magnificent redwood out the corner window. I am always delighted to see how the light adds its gold to green leaves, breaks up the blue gray rain sky with slivers of silver, glints of white. The presence of the tree helps me to stay focused, even as I sometimes long for a view of mountains or hills.

The windows in my life are a consistent invitation to explore, to let my mind travel even when I need to stay put. My windows remind me that there is a marvelous world outside this little study where I sit at the computer too much of the time. I remember the small bedroom in the house I rented for so many years with casement windows facing east toward the Berkeley hills, like the closet-size room I had when I was a student in Florence and my window faced toward the Tuscan hill town of Fiesole. I loved flinging open the windows to the day, greeting the morning, taking a moment to breathe in and look out toward the blue green hills.

To think that windows are unimportant, to imagine we can survive in windowless rooms, to think we can live without beauty, is part of the craziness of our time. When we are at work and at school, our eyes need to travel, to rest for a moment on a green leaf, to remember the sun's journey through the heavens. We need the air's caress, the companionship of sound, the play of light.

The writer Michael Ventura describes the window into beauty that changed his life when he was a skinny, fever-wracked boy. He recalls that most of that time seems like a dream, but the reality of the window remains vivid many years later. "For several days and nights, too weak to lift my head, all my attention was fixed on that window. It was . . . just a window. But pigeons would alight on the sill, suddenly, as though out of nowhere. They would make their clucking and cooing sounds. Occasionally, one would simply sit very still for a long time. Then, just as inexplicably, fall off. Through that window I would watch the changing light of the sky, and the clouds—I had never noticed how many shades of light inhabited the sky. And sometimes a flock of pigeons would sail across my field of vision, high up and far away. Sometimes, too, their wings would catch the sun as they banked all together at some unseen mutual signal, and that flash of many-winged light thrilled my heart.

"I think I remember that window so well because it was my first consciousness of beauty—that is, my first independent, deeply inner meeting between the beauty of the world and my soul. All my former contexts had been shattered, I could hardly even move, I was in a sense utterly on my own, yet even in this state (or because of this state?) I was being touched directly by a sweet and transforming force, or feeling, for which I know no other word but beauty. I was many years away from the concepts of contemplation and meditation, but I believe now that those were the fundamental elements, or activities, of my enthrallment, my rapt attention, as I focused upon that window. It's impossible to prove, but I believe that my intake, my inspiration (literally, my breathing in) of the elegance, the beauty of the birds and the sky, gave me strength and saved my life."

Art: Mirror & Window

Looking at art can be as necessary, as nourishing as opening the window, as inspecting one's soul through the eyes looking back in the mirror. Art offers a window that opens into self and other. Not a literal window as in a Matisse painting, but an opening that allows us to look outside ourselves, into ourselves. Art reflects and transmits light and dark, spirit and soul, awareness, the invigorating, refreshing challenge of new vision.

Art helps us see beyond where we are, into the mind and time of someone else. The same piece of art travels in more than one direction, takes us to more than one destination, offers several stops along the way.

Nobody else sees the world as we do. Perhaps that is part of the human need to create—out of the need to be understood and the need to understand. Out of immense loneliness, wonder, and great joy we are moved to communicate, to translate and distill the experience of what we have seen and heard and felt, to explore and extend what we know. Especially at this time when so much art seems divorced from spiritual context, art still carries soul, still continues to instruct, to translate, to communicate from one part to another, from one of us to another.

No one paints the same picture. No one tells the same story. Each of us is different. Each of us offers a story that is one piece of the Great Story. Each of us, a cell in the body of God.

At a painting workshop, I look at a wall full of drawings. Twenty people have been assigned to take a stone and make a picture out of relationship to that stone, and when I look at our drawings, it is so clear that our seeing is not simply a question of style or of technical or intellectual preferences. One person draws the image of the hand around the rock, another offers the feeling of the rock inside the hand. We perceive and sense, attend to and know the world differently. For some the stone is solid, the granddaughter of boulders, and then the world is well defined. Someone else tells us about a stone made of dancing atoms, whirling, blurring colors, informing us the world she inhabits is mostly space. In these drawings of rock, made from one day of seeing, we see who is attracted to the sensual and earthy, the abundant life of the stone, in whose work an austere stone speaks of deep emotional longing.

A few days later I find myself looking at a classroom wall with twenty different portraits of George Washington rendered by second graders, and then later that day, as I am waiting for my car to be repaired, looking at a magazine layout of sixteen faces of Jesus gathered from all over the world. I see the white-haired Founding Father in each portrait of George Washington. I recognize the

Notes on the Need for Beauty

essence of Jesus as I look at the face of the Korean Jesus, the African Jesus, the red-haired Jesus, the golden prophet, a feminine Jesus. George Washington is still George Washington, and Jesus is still Jesus. George Washington is also a portrait of the little boy who made it; Jesus wears the face of the people who pray to him. It never ceases to amaze me how much of ourselves we put into the pictures we make.

Again, for a time, like that six-year-old self looking at her friend in the mirror, I want to look at the world from the eyes of someone else—a scholarly Chinese landscape painter, the Egyptian mystic who painted the simple faces of the *Gnostic Book of Hours*, the second grader who gave George Washington her eyebrows. Although I can't look through others' eyes, I can look at the records that they have left, and for a moment I feel like I am standing next to them, they are beside me, and we are looking at the world together. For a moment I leave what I know and travel to other places, other times.

Looking at art I become a pilgrim traveling across a bridge strung with lanterns. Looking at art we become scholars traveling across centuries to centers of understanding that we weren't sure we still believed in. No one can tell us how to look at art, although at times experts—teachers and scholars, critics and philosophers—can offer clues or send us back to look again. Art documents the experience of soul across cultures. Like seeds from an ancient tomb that sprout centuries later, certain images live long after their makers have died. The artist gives us her vision and her imagination, transforming it into shapes and colors, textures and lines, and we receive the gift, not through detached analysis but through our own vision, our own imagination. The eye of the heart is nourished by what carries life.

I put two prints on the wall near the window in my office. A painting of Mary Magdalene by the French painter Georges de La Tour, and next to that picture a Vermeer painting, also from the 1600s. La Tour's subject was light, especially the way we are outlined by light in the dark, how candlelight emphasizes the edges of things. And in this painting, *The Penitent Magdalene*, she sits in the dark, one hand on her cheek, one hand on a skull. A mirror reflects not her pensive face, but the skull, lit from behind by a single flame. The glow is everywhere. In the dark room, in her light face, in the dim mirror reminding us of the finiteness of our physical existence.

In the Vermeer, an anonymous Dutch woman stands in a dark blue dress bending toward the window, one hand on its frame, one hand on a gleaming pitcher, the world above her shoulder in the form of an olive-tinted map. Vermeer's emblems—the woman, the map, the window—have become well-known. His subject, like La Tour's, is also, always light; his is the intimate light of the everyday. The room sings with light. It illuminates the bright surface of the pitcher, the woman's serene face, the beautifully painted windowpanes. When I go to New York, I discover these two pictures a few rooms apart at the Met, and I spend an afternoon moving back and forth between these pictures, the Vermeer much smaller than I imagine, the La Tour larger, astonished all over again by real paint and real looking.

Maps and skulls, pitchers and candles, windows and mirrors. One image as practical and daily as the other is dark and romantic. Yet both are filled with silence, both are filled with light. I couldn't begin to know which one is more mysterious. And both are beautiful.

Beauty Secrets, Love Stories

Love is a yearning that comes from the heart
from a flowing over of great beauty;
and the eyes are the first to give it birth,
and the heart gives itself for bread.

Jacopo da Lentini
translated by Gioia Timpanelli

Our hearts yearn for beauty. In the Kabbalah, beauty, called *tiferet*, is where spirit and form meet and the human and divine are in balance. Linked to compassion and harmony, beauty is at the very center of the Tree of Life.

In Wim Wenders's eloquent film *Wings of Desire*, an angel falls in love with a beautiful airborne trapeze artist and chooses to become a man, at the same time falling into life and delighting in its substantiality. Despite his wisdom, the angel has never known what it is like to experience the joy and suffering of physical existence. Once he lands on earth, he finds life immediately different than he has imagined, and in the film the elegant black-and-white of eternity becomes the brash color of our time. In his first moments as a human, he bleeds and exclaims that blood has taste, he feels the weight of a stone, he breathes in the cold air and rubs his hands together to warm himself. He identifies the color red and excitedly confirms his discovery with a passerby. So many things we take for granted are strange and wonderful to him, and with exuberance and innocence he begins to figure out how to make the transition from witness to participant. In the wholeness of human experience he praises love, "true in the day and true in the night." By falling in love with a woman, the angel has fallen in love with the beauty of the world.

My cousin gives her young daughter a doll around the time her new brother is born, and the two-and-a-half-year-old asks if the doll is beautiful. "What do you think?" "The doll is beautiful because he is nice." For the child, it is simple—love goes together with beauty. Her mother says, "I want my daughter to think that I am beautiful. I want my daughter to know that she is beautiful."

Another woman tells me, "My mother did a lot of things wrong. She was an alcoholic, and she had a very hard life. But she always told us we were beautiful. So there I am, trying on bathing suits after giving birth to three children, and I'm the only woman in the dressing rooms not moaning about my body."

It is rare for people to learn that they are beautiful when they are young. Many learn that they are not beautiful, that only a few are beautiful. There are a variety of reasons for this. The elegant woman who grew up in the shadow of her handsome, golden brother, "the beauty of the family," recalls, half a century later, her mother telling her she was an "ugly baby." How could her mother, who as a teenager growing up in Norway was harassed by Nazis, feel that it was safe for her daughter's beauty to shine?

Another remembers that her mother's refrain through adolescence was, "You would be really beautiful . . . if you would wear makeup. You would be really beautiful . . . if you fixed your hair. You would be really beautiful . . . if you lost some weight." In her twenties, the young woman replies, tentatively, "I am beautiful," and stops her mother in her tracks.

As I look at images of young women in fashion magazines and

pictures in a book of people farming, there is something I am trying to understand about two-dimensional images and three-dimensional presences, the dance between inner and outer, the relationship between appearance, harmony, beauty, and respect. Sometimes it feels like these images are in the air; they wrap around us like ribbons. In Michael Ableman's book *From the Good Earth: A Celebration of Growing Food around the World*, the farmers, young and old, male and female, working alone and together, growing rice, planting peas, winnowing beans, photographed against sky and field, carry extraordinary beauty in their diverse forms and movements. Without romanticizing their toil, there is something about people being as they are instead of trying to appear a certain way that is arresting, in the way that beauty is arresting, summoning our attention. The photographer's desire to understand how farming is a "natural bond between community and generous earth" infuses these photographs with a beauty that is substantial, essential, and almost tangible.

In contrast, most of the photographs of young women in fashion magazines today look unreal, fantastic, vacant. Every month these magazines offer up their beauty secrets, often quantified as if to prove their authority: "28 Ways to Improve Your Skin," "How to Lose 30 Pounds in 30 Days," "Top 10 Plastic Surgeons." As the media equates beauty with youth and sex appeal, we are faced with impossible ideals for what women (and men) should look like. We live in a world where billions of dollars are spent changing the ways we look, and millions of dollars are spent advertising ways "to look" so that we are looked at. The billboards, the ads, the magazine covers, the models and actresses present us with improbable images of beauty, created under the surgeon's knife, refined through hours and hours of beauty treatments, manipulated by sophisticated computer programs. The subtext of these endlessly recycled stories is that attaining beauty will bring us happiness and make us lovable. We are powerfully affected by these images; that's the purpose and skill of them. Yet the love we are yearning for, the ability to let things matter and people affect us deeply, depends on a vulnerability and openness we are often busy avoiding by attempting to create such impenetrable surfaces.

In our society, we inhale the emphasis on female beauty like the air we breathe. In the last forty years, as the territory of masculinity and femininity has been turned inside out, we have been endlessly obsessed with the nature of gender, the question of what is innate and what is cultural, what is normal and what is possible. Sometimes, frustrated with the discussion, I remember a reference I once heard to "the adjacent sex," rather than "the opposite sex," or the truth expressed by the Japanese poet Ikkyu:

> *As to the skin*
> *what a difference*
> *between a man and a woman.*
> *But as to the bones*
> *both are simply human beings.*

Yet if we talk about beauty without acknowledging how differently men and women are raised to consider their appearance, we ignore the very real ways that women have been trained to appear, and that men have been trained to look at women. Historically, beauty has been an avenue to power for many women at times when other roads were blocked, but it has often been dangerous and lonely for women who are called beautiful, just as it has been dangerous and lonely for women who are called ugly. As women, we are raised to take pride in our appearance, and then put down as superficial for caring so much about how we look. And many men have been raised to confuse attractiveness with goodness, to see the image of perfection in a deeply flawed soul, or to find imperfection in a woman who is much more complex than a perfect image. Many men remain exiled from their beauty because they think it's a quality of women; women are exiled from beauty because they think it belongs to only a few.

As we absorb the images of female beauty that society presents, we are comparing our faces and bodies to those of women who don't even exist, though the resulting epidemic of self-hate among women is very real. In cartoons and on sitcoms, in therapy offices and among friends, sometimes half joking, sometimes with great anguish, women express violent dislike of parts of ourselves, tremendous pain about the shape of our forms. Elementary school girls with eating disorders, models in magazines cheerfully proclaiming their "flaws," disrespect for older women are all symptoms of our loathing. The problem is so common it's a cliché, and yet to stay with the suffering, to face the amount of time and energy spent trying to change one's appearance, is clearly necessary. When we have so thoroughly rejected who we are, how do we begin to return to our true selves?

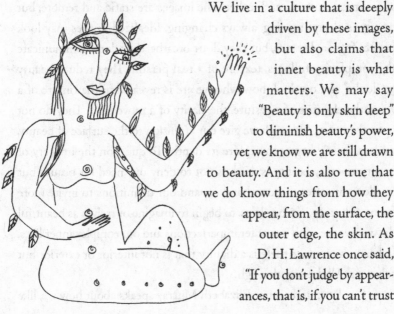

We live in a culture that is deeply driven by these images, but also claims that inner beauty is what matters. We may say "Beauty is only skin deep" to diminish beauty's power, yet we know we are still drawn to beauty. And it is also true that we do know things from how they appear, from the surface, the outer edge, the skin. As D. H. Lawrence once said, "If you don't judge by appearances, that is, if you can't trust the impression which things make on you, you're a fool." We do need to trust our impressions, the way things appear to us. Sometimes incorrectly but often truly, we sense the outer form as an extension of the inner being. It is certainly not our only way of knowing, but it is where we start, and it is basic, connected with our intuition and imagination. We also know that our own impressions, our own reactions, have been strongly influenced by the culture that surrounds us, the images that we have digested. Because these images both reflect the culture and instruct us in how to arrange ourselves and interpret our lives, it is valuable to look at them again. It is valuable to ask: Who created these images and why? Where in our bodies do we take them in? How have our delight in decoration and display, our longings and dreams been shaped and manipulated?

One problem with these images is that they emphasize sight at the expense of our other senses, leave out the way the air becomes alive as we move closer to each other. The images are static and remote, but beauty is always moving, always changing. Idealized images may look perfect from a distance, but they don't breathe, they don't communicate the complexity, fullness, texture of a real person. They reduce beauty to "looks" and overlook how who we are is revealed in the timbre of a voice, the elegance of a gesture, the clarity of a movement. They do not open the heart. Although we give our attention to the surface of beauty, we have barely begun to explore its depth. To question the imagery of beauty, the way beauty is used, is not to deny our need for beauty but to allow ourselves to extend and expand our definitions to invite more forms of beauty into our lives, to begin to imagine ourselves as beautiful the way we are, with our outer imperfections and our complex inner lives. In beauty's presence there is a dignity that is not interior or exterior but coherent. All the way through.

Gardener and author Elizabeth Murray speaks about how we, like flowers, are here to be beautiful. Grounded in the intricate interdependence and beauty of the world of plants and insects, she sees that our beauty is a gift to each other, a part of the cyclical and ephemeral natural world. As we begin to explore how fluid our appearances are, minute to minute and over a lifetime, the interconnection between perception and expression, between liveliness and beauty, becomes more visible. We remember that beauty is a quality of radiance, luminosity, and coherence that inspires our attention. Beauty is within and around us, ordinary and extraordinary.

It has taken me years to come to the edge of these matters, to consider how our own beauty is both a "given" and a choice that requires courage and generosity to accept. To honor the impulse toward beauty even as its image is distorted and manipulated. It's not enough to lament the tyranny of mainstream media and culture. How do we move beyond these images and begin to cultivate, appreciate, and acknowledge a more inclusive sense of beauty?

Ornamentation & Tenderness

Our animal selves delight in embellishment and display; we decorate ourselves and feather our nests. At root our interest and obsession with appearance is an extension of our desire for subtle and sophisticated communication. Visual communication is an extremely important part of human interaction, but it's not separate from other forms of language and gesture, who we are and what we are trying to say. It is a part of the dance, a form of exchange.

The art historian Sylvia Ardyn Boone, who observed women in the Mende culture in Sierra Leone, explains the enormous significance of their grooming rituals. "As Westerners," she writes, "it is difficult for us to appreciate the communicative power Mende attribute to women's hair. The hair must be well-groomed; merely to be presentable, a woman's hair must be clean, oiled, and plaited. For the sake of elegance and sexual appeal, hair must be shaped into beautiful and complicated styles . . . Offering to plait another woman's hair is a way of asking her to become your friend . . . one woman saying to another: 'I like you. I appreciate you. I have thought about you enough to imagine a style that will suit and enhance your features. I am not jealous of you. I want you to look beautiful so that you will attract love, admiration, and all the good that these bring. I am willing to stand or bend for several hours, working on your hair, expecting no remuneration. My sacrifice proves that I want only the best for you.' Thus, braiding someone's hair is indicative of ideal care and love, the concrete contribution of one woman to the success of another."

All over the world, men and women decorate and beautify, dress up for themselves, each other, for parties and celebrations, festivals and holy days. The textile scholar Nora Fisher writes in her book *Mud, Mirror and Thread*: "In India, ornament, adornment and indeed decoration of all varieties continue to find an exhilarated acceptance, one that has spanned over 5,000 years. A plain cloth is adorned with embroidery; a mud wall or floor with mud paint or rice flour; a mud pot with slip or relief embellishment; a stone with a red dot. A woman might wear dozens of pieces of jewelry and many elaborately embroidered garments. A man prepared for a festive occasion might have painted fingernails in addition to jewelry and an elaborate hairdo and headdress. All of these elements of adornment have deep significance."

As Fisher articulates the creativity and playfulness that emerge when humans decorate ourselves, our tools, and our environments, she highlights the spiritual nature of the practice, quoting the great Indian art historian and philosopher Ananda Coomaraswamy: "We must not think of ornament as something added to an object which might have been ugly without it. The beauty of anything unadorned is not increased by ornament, but made more effective by it. Ornament is characterization; ornaments are attributes . . . It is generally by means of what we call its decoration that a thing is ritually transformed and made to function spiritually as well as physically." Or, as James Trilling writes in *The Language of Ornament*, "The power of beauty is also the power to glorify."

Certainly, tending one's appearance is about presenting self to others, but it is also a taking care of self. The love story between the body and the soul is expressed through acts of grooming and embellishment. We are nourishing our bodies and our senses when we choose a hair conditioner, a scent, a gorgeous undergarment, a pair of glamorous red sandals or comfortable brown socks. Polishing the face, brushing our own hair, can be like petting a cat, a soothing, relaxing, curious attention to self, healthful and honoring. Embellishment becomes a way of looking after oneself, honoring the body, remembering the senses, the pathway between our inner and outer worlds. The body's natural majesty and magnificence are so often forgotten in our daily lives, but beauty thrives on attention, which is why these rituals are so important. They send a message to and through the body. The ingredients can be delicious:

strawberry, cucumber, honey, milk, almond oil, lavender, citrus, vanilla. Scent, like color, like sound, soothes us and wakes us up.

A woman in her fifties confesses her adolescent beauty secrets. When she was a teenager preparing to go out, she daubed vanilla on her wrists because the scent delighted her, put orange peels in the garbage disposal so the air would be filled with the fragrance of fresh citrus. When her date would arrive, she appeared to waft in on the scent of orange and vanilla. Maybe it's not only the three-step beauty regimen but the time we are devoting to taking care of ourselves that makes the skin shine. Feeling more alive, our mood shifts; is it any surprise that we look different?

Grooming and ornamenting the self ground us to earth. By sharing the intimacies of a dressing room, the rituals of manicures and pedicures, facials and massages, sometimes making "small talk," complaining about our lives, telling our stories, or revealing our dreams, we can experience a kind of tender attention, outside our daily routines. We are tended and soothed, polished, sometimes purified. In the poem "Secrets of the Old Cuban Women," Erasmo Vasquez writes how once, visiting family friends in Miami, he glances into a room and sees an old friend of his mother's standing and brushing his mother's hair. Tenderness is a true beauty secret that exists between friend and friend, between parent and child, as well as between lovers. It is nurtured within relationships between self and others, not bought or sold on the recommendation of a magazine.

A Meditation on Love

When people talk about where they find beauty,
what is beautiful to them, they reveal whom they
love and how they love, and what they love to do.
Listening as people recollect and offer their
own beauty stories, I am in awe of the ways
that beauty moves in our lives. Everyone who has
a family, or loves an animal or a place or a piece of music, has
a beauty story to tell. A man reflects on the challenge of keeping Eros alive
in a long marriage, a woman speaks of what it was like to grow up with a
mother who was a model, another comments on learning how to appreciate her own beauty when compared to a classically gorgeous sister.

As we speak about our personal relationship to beauty and what
is beautiful to us, we reveal our longings to be seen, our need for acceptance, the powerful influence of mothers and fathers, grandparents, older
siblings, first loves and favorite cousins, our keen ability to remember what
embarrassed, confused, and delighted us, our yearnings to stand out and
to fit in, our desire to be loved. In our own stories we mark the distinction
between looking beautiful and feeling beautiful—the part of us trapped
by our culture and the part of us that knows our own value.

A nurse declares that her beauty secret is that the husband who
adores her is nearsighted, so when she is close enough for him to see her,
he is seeing her with the eyes of love. A newspaper story describes how a
young interracial blind couple got together when she became attracted to
his voice, reminding us that prejudice is born in dismissing people because
they look different, because we see them as exotic and frightening.

"Love is blind," we say, but perhaps it is more accurate to say love sees with different eyes. Love sees beyond the surface. Love opens the door for beauty. When we see with the eye, we develop the ability to refine, to judge, to discriminate. When we see with the heart, we expand the view of what it is to be human, see the common dream, see the wisdom of friends and neighbors, see there is no separation between that which is most beautiful and the everyday world. The eye of the heart sees with a wholeness that allows imperfections and idiosyncrasies to coexist with beauty. The eye of the heart knows surface and depth are not opposites. Beauty is a process, a revelation, not a finished state.

Beauty reveals itself over time in relationship. The people I love are beautiful to me. I'm not sure if my eyes are blinded by love or it is love that lets me see their beauty. Knowing them over time, my appreciation of who they are and how they appear increases. Their beauty comes from their liveliness and authentic sweetness, their intention to live lives that make some sense (and some nonsense), the spirited coherence of being who they are.

A teacher recalls sitting in on another teacher's class and thinking, "Isn't it strange how ordinary looking, how rather plain these kids are? My students are beautiful." She sees her students as gorgeous because she knows them well. "When you sit with them or work with them and see them every day and know their moods, they become more amazing, not less so," she says. "And then, I realized that the kids in the other classroom look beautiful to their teacher, too."

When a beautician notes, "All my clients are beautiful," I hear how her awareness of and attention to beauty brings it out in others.

When we are most alive, we are beautiful. When we are in love, we are reminded that we are beautiful. And sometimes when we know we are beautiful, we find ourselves in love. "In love" usually means the romantic sense of being with one other person who in that moment we feel reflects us perfectly. In love, living in the field of love. Sometimes I have felt like I was in love, even when there was no one I was in love with. I couldn't talk about my lover's hands or eyes or voice. I couldn't focus all this love on one other, and it was both confusing and revealing to realize how much we become places for each other to rest in. Alone and "in love" it is easy to feel like you're making it up. Our songs and movies have told us such great sentimental stories about being "in love," we forget that being in love can be a state of truth as well as an illusion.

Longtime friends witnessing a friend "falling in love" often caution the infatuated person that being in love is a dizzy, temporary state. I think of this territory not just as a delicious romantic dance, but as a field to which we can travel from many places. There is a way in which being in love with anything—a person, a place, a project—is crossing a border into a country where the ego does not rule, being in a state where essence is honored. We are both inside and outside our everyday selves. It is always interesting to observe what happens when we return to the land of ordinary life. Can we live with more generosity and trust?

I never want to underestimate the capacity that being "in love" has to change our seeing, expand our vision, and remind us of both human beauty and human frailty. The search for the beloved is full of paradoxes. We want to be who we are when we are our best self, and sometimes because we have met that self when we are in love, we believe that self only exists in the presence of the other. So we hold on to the other and lose ourselves, forget that love is partly of this world and partly of some other place.

An old beau spoke of the danger of trying to make our lovers be God, insisting that we each need our own relationship to the Source. It sounded logical, but I rebelled at his analysis. In this world, one of the ways we glimpse God is when we are in love. Not that the beloved is God, but that God is the Beloved, a tradition as old as the Song of Songs and the ecstatic poems of wandering Indian mystics, the Sufis. One of the most beautiful and accessible ways to address God is as Love.

The Greeks gave us the image of Eros, the unpredictable archer before whom even the Gods trembled. Hindus tell their stories of the Gopi maidens seeking Krishna, the bewitchingly beautiful, blue-skinned god; Krishna with his soft glowing eyes, perfumed hair, Krishna drawing women to him, touching each in forgotten registers of being.

What is done with love is done in beauty to celebrate the God that loves. More and more I believe the messengers of love, the envoys and the couriers of beauty are everywhere. And I wonder how something so clear can also be mysterious. The Indian poet Ghalib writes, "This earth, burnished by hearing the Name, is so certain of Love that the sky bends unceasingly down, to greet its own light."

In meeting the beloved, we experience a tremendous amount of contact between the outer reality of two people and the inner person each evokes in the other. It is fashionable now to dismiss this exchange as projection, when it is a calling forth out of ghosts and fog and deep longings. It is humbling to realize how much we are dreaming each other, calling each other out of our solitary rooms into the post office lines and sidewalk cafés and conference halls where we bump into each other, notice each other, begin to speak. How can we find ourselves except by seeking, losing and finding each other, losing and finding ourselves? What is so close is hidden better than the treasures we search for everywhere. Such a serious search requires "great foolishness." We lose ourselves, find ourselves in each other, glimpse our own radiance, run away and return. Sometimes it seems like what we are looking for is so deep within us we have no choice but to look for it outside.

I have always loved tales of courtship, the stories of how dear friends and lovers find each other, because so often these meetings are utterly unlikely. While our attention is elsewhere, the Friend, the Guest, the Companion, the Beloved sneaks up out of nowhere. Sometimes one of us recognizes the connection before the other is ready; sometimes we linger around the edges of each other's lives before we can move to the center. Sometimes we have crossed paths many times before we finally speak. When we do meet, when we recognize each other, we are both utterly surprised and not surprised at all. One says, "You have come after so long," and the other says, "I came as fast as I could."

There is no way to anticipate when these meetings will occur in the outer world, and yet there are many preparations that can be made. And when we do meet the beloved in the world, whether it's for seven months or twenty years or ten lifetimes, the sweetness spills out and overflows, infusing everything—the five-year-old boys picking pears, an old rose tree, the sky at dawn, so much music. The gifts are everywhere. What was ordinary and unremarkable becomes incredibly dear. Trembling and tender, we spill out of ourselves, become intoxicated with the beauty that surrounds us.

And although we recognize and remember the connection, we don't know what form it will take; often when we try to fit it into the forms we know or have inherited, the form doesn't work and we end up disappointed, disillusioned, unable to understand why love has failed us or we have failed love. Whether love survives the transition into the everyday rhythms of work and obligation, or simply breaks us open to the longing for wholeness, the longing to live more holy, we have tasted something we will always know and always forget.

Love becomes a cloth two people weave together; threading and stitching connection we weave it and it weaves itself out of us—a blanket to cover the bed, a tablecloth on which we put food, shirts worn close to the heart. Velvet and coarse cotton, linen, silk, old denim.

As a character, Love appears in our lives in any number of guises, disguises. In the old Joni Mitchell song, Love shows up with his sleeping roll and a madman's soul. The medieval writer Mechthild of Magdeburg records a dialogue between Love and Soul in which Soul says: "Lady Love, you have taken from me all that I ever possessed on earth," and Love replies, "But Lady Queen, what a blessed exchange!"

When Love comes to our school, we are all new students. There is no preparing ahead of time. Love sets in motion so many forces. Sometimes we accept love cheerfully, sometimes offer ourselves grudgingly, humbly, because what we most hope for, we also fear. Liberated and bound through love, we choose and we are chosen; the choice is never wholly ours.

I feel skeptical when people hold out their crisp lists of what they want in a lover or a spouse, as if our visions of relationship can simply be articulated like a job description with specific requirements, as if we can classify, catalogue, and rank all our longings, our needs, our gifts. What we offer each other is often very different from what we say we are looking for. We grow through knowing each other. We grow through being alone and yearning for each other. Especially at a time when many intimate relationships seem fragile, it takes courage to see the beauty in relation-ship, relationship as a path of beauty. We meet in beauty and then must discover how to keep the beauty between us alive.

How do we develop the courage and clarity to tend the fire after we have discovered its radiance and heat? Finding love is one thing: re-finding love, refining love, letting ourselves be refined by love is something else. More than we can know, our task is to learn to experience love, to cultivate the rhythms of patience that love requires.

What the soul requires to become whole is deeper and more radiant than our personal agendas and histories, greater than the summaries of what we say we want. Yet, it is not to dismiss our dreams but to listen more attentively to what lives beneath these first yearnings. What we say we want is only a beginning. As Rumi says, "We have ways with each other that will never be known by anyone."

Companions, the ones we break bread with; conspirators who breathe together. Best friends. Bedfellows. Witness, associate, ally, colleague. *Confrère, compère, comadre, compadre.* Suitor, beau, sweetheart, spouse. Consort, cohort, dear one, sweet pea, honey, cupcake, babe.

One night when musing with a group of us about what he would do if he had several other lives to live, a sculptor says he would like to be a bar of a soap in a women's gym. A woman sitting next to him informs him that the soap in the women's gym comes in liquid form, not in bars. A lively discussion ensues about the value of such a brief life. Months later I find out that they are "seeing each other." Eros all around us, surrounds us. In the words of the Spanish poet Juan Ramón Jiménez, "God desiring and desired." Or as a fifth grader wrote, "The river is curious to meet the ocean. The ocean is curious to be mud."

The mythic and the personal intersect in our love lives. The inner face of the beloved is revealed in the forms he or she wears in our outer lives. At times I have felt like I was in a dream in which I meet the same person in many different disguises. It's not that any one face is a false face or a mask, but that the beloved may move through our lives in very

91

mysterious ways. I love the old stories in which the beloved is partly of the human world, partly of the animal kingdom, and things are not quite what they seem. In love the god becomes a man, the wild one is tamed, the fierce one is the most gentle, the ugly one carries true beauty. The woman is tested by the Goddess. Or she marries a bear. Or he marries a seal. They travel beyond all the disguises and masks to risk the nobility of true beauty. Sometimes they journey inward within the soul, and sometimes the journey is played out in the world with great flourish and drama. Sometimes there is a sadness in deep love, a sadness at the center of joy because love, like birth and death, breaks open the heart, breaks open the dream of beauty to reveal some other beauty, bigger and wilder and more precious than we knew. These love stories are not about "love at first sight" or "happily ever after." They are layered tales of grief and patience, courage and transformation.

In our own lives we play so many of the parts. At times the one we are looking for is close by, and yet we must travel a great distance to find him or her. At times we are the one who must wait, without help or hope, while the beloved is sent into exile. Longing carries us further than we ever could have imagined. We try to talk our way out of our separate predicaments, but while we are powerless to help each other, help appears nonetheless because we are so sincere. To have faith in fate, to be helpless and dependent on each other—if one thinks about it, the whole endeavor seems impossible. Yet, one attempts it anyway, going forward step by step into the unknown, in the dark, in the light, to meet the beloved, to become more whole.

The beauty we seek in relationship and in the world is both more ordinary and more precious than we usually imagine, more safe and more dangerous, often both less dramatic and far more unpredictable. What happens when we invite in a more rigorous beauty, a chaotic, lively beauty that isn't afraid of strong feeling or insistent on intensity? Such beauty is wild and sweet; it wakes us up to our own aliveness, our own wildness, our own sweetness. Beauty doesn't live in us so much as between us and through us.

Love Letters to the Earth

When I was young and reading love poetry, I wanted all the love poems to be written to one other person, reflecting a relationship of incredible richness and diversity. Two people who have many different relationships with each other. I didn't realize how many forms love takes, both within and outside our inherited traditions of romantic love. I didn't realize how love between two people requires others, certainly human but perhaps other others—ancestors and spirits of the land.

We offer love poems to the breathtakingly beautiful mountains and to a small hill where we walk at the end of the day. Love letters between body and earth, stone and star, cypress and cedar, citrus and rose. Love poems praise the heron standing on the island in the lake at dusk at the edge of the distant shore, the unexpected owls at sunset. The air is full of voices. The Mystery calls back: You do not live here alone.

One of my favorite love stories tells of a mountain who is befriended by a bird. Each year the bird visits briefly on her way to finding a place to build her nest. The mountain is enchanted by the bright singing and liveliness of the bird, and wants her to stay. The bird knows she can't survive on the desolate mountain and is aware of how brief a bird's life is, but she promises to return each spring and sing to the mountain for the rest of her life. She will name one of her daughters Joy and instruct her how to find the mountain. "And she will name a daughter Joy also, and tell her how to find you. And she will name a daughter Joy also, and tell her how to find you. Each Joy will have a daughter Joy, so that no matter how many years pass, you will always have a friend to greet you and fly above you and sing to you."

Years go by, and the mountain becomes more and more attached to the bird, so that each year it is harder for the mountain to watch the bird leave. After ninety-nine years, as the bird disappears into the sky, the mountain's heart breaks, and the mountain's tears become a small stream. When the bird appears the following spring, the mountain only weeps and cannot talk to her. The next year the bird brings a tiny seed to plant close to the stream. The root of the small plant breaks through the hard rock, drawing food from the softening ground, sending a shoot into the sunlight. For several springs, the bird brings seeds, and the mountain weeps. Softened stone turns to soil, grasses and flowering plants sprout near the stream, insects appear. Eventually the rocky mountain has turned into a fertile green place where birds can make a home, and the bird comes to stay at last.

A wise friend comments, "We do the broken-heart love thing because it's the fertile soul-soil for new life. Just as bringing a child into the world tears a woman's body, breaking the heart open changes our lives in ways we could never anticipate." Much as I sometimes fight it, this is the deal here: we learn from both joy and disappointment. There is a necessity to our loneliness, a powerful teaching in the grief that waters and washes and purifies us.

When the heart opens with affection for the world we live in, we sense how much of the time we live cut off. How love changes us is so literal, literal and gradual. It is the rocky hard mountain heart softened over time until it becomes a place where Joy can live, love can thrive, beauty can make a home.

Describing the trombonist Julian Priester improvising a solo suite to his recently born son, the poet David Meltzer writes, "The resonance of his trombone tones filled the white-walled space with a deep burnished offering of intensely articulate tenderness." Such music is possible only when the heart expands beyond its cage and bursts out with affection, an affection that ultimately embraces the world, undivided, the self not separate.

Where do we find instructions about tenderness, learn to read the love poems and letters that we are writing all the time without even knowing it? In the language of union and separation, in the grammar of the heart, in the alphabet of ecstasy, there is delicacy and boldness, breakup and breakthrough, radiance and immense soul-polishing beauty.

We need to attend more to the love stories in our own lives, so much more eccentric and idiosyncratic than we know. Even the most unassuming people have tender stories to tell: two cousins who were little girls together growing up next door in Brooklyn, now in their seventies, live across the street from each other in Manhattan. Every night as it grows dark, they flash lights between their apartments to signal they are home. A man maintains ties with his ex-girlfriend's children long after the couple's romantic relationship has ended. A friend I rarely see is in town the weekend a beloved cat is dying, and as I tend to this close animal friend, my old friend tends to me. Our own love stories are rich with texture and subtlety, rich with soulfulness and beauty.

My neighbor sighs that the love stories we see in the movies have about as much to do with "showing us the real relationships in our lives as the beauty magazines have to do with what we look like," and are equally insidious. So many of the images and narratives of our culture amp up passion and drama, our fairy tales and films often end where our real relationships begin. Brought up on happy endings and sad love songs, we must learn together to navigate this new territory, to cultivate affection in daily life. Like any art form, love teaches us to lean into the unknown, to develop the capacity to be strong and receptive, to tell the beloved: "I never saw you until I loved you."

Too often we try to live our love stories in such a narrow way; sometimes the love story we are in the middle of living is much bigger than personal love. More and more I recognize, I remember that we are always in relationship, in a conversation that calls forth the greater self. The more we participate and engage, the more beauty exists within, between, among us. This great love enlarges our intelligence and educates the heart, expands the lungs with a capacity to love the world, a tenderness and affection that fill us with beauty.

"If we look more closely at beauty and try to describe more carefully the beauty of the world," writes psychologist Robert Sardello, in *Love and the World*, "we do not arrive at aesthetics, but rather at love. Is not beauty the particular way in which the world expresses itself as love?"

In recent years, ecologists have begun to speak about "biophilia," the love of life for life. Yes, even the backyard is a jungle, the tiny parts of the garden we don't see, the ladybugs and spiders, the water striders, moving through it all in a great procession. Perhaps it is our love for earth and other animals, our belonging to life, that offers the biggest beauty secret of all.

Beauty & Other Forbidden Qualities

> Beauty is startling. She wears a gold shawl in the summer and
> sells seven kinds of honey at the flea market. She is young and old
> at once, my daughter and my grandmother. In school she excelled
> in mathematics and poetry. She doesn't anger easily but she was
> annoyed with the journalist who kept asking about her favorites—
> as if beauty had one favorite color or one favorite flower. She doesn't
> mind questions and she is fond of riddles. Beauty will dance with
> anyone who is brave enough to ask her.
>
> from *The Book of Qualities*

While I was developing a play based on *The Book of Qualities*, the actors were comfortable and effective portraying qualities such as Grief, Greed, Jealousy. When we came to noble qualities such as Honor or Truth, their performances became more wooden, as though these qualities belonged to saints, not ordinary people. I wanted Beauty and Ugliness to be played by the same person, to demonstrate that at times they change places with each other as they borrow our faces. An actress who by all "objective" standards was very beautiful read the personification of Ugliness with great conviction and verve. She shrank into her body as she read Beauty, her voice became thinner and more pretentious. Afterward, she confessed she felt like a fraud reading Beauty.

Beauty becomes a forbidden quality because most of us feel it can't belong to us. Whom does it belong to? Animals and children and glamorous young models. No one is allowed to be beautiful for long. A therapist who has worked with severe abuse notes, "Children have a lot of light when they come into the world; it is as if they're still looking at God's face. Sometimes people threatened by that light try to grab it for themselves, causing much harm in the process."

A mother admires how her daughter receives compliments, her two-and-a-half-year-old's self-assurance. "When grown-ups tell Bonnie she has beautiful eyes, she says, 'Yes, I do.' People are taken aback. Bonnie Devon likes herself. It's acceptable now, but we aren't comfortable with it when girls are older."

Often we distrust people who accept their beauty rather than deny it, as if to acknowledge one's beauty is to arouse the anger of the gods, as if to say one is beautiful is to say that one is God. It seems like a confabulation of inner and outer, of ego and essence. On some level we know we are each a piece of the divine, we are a small part of this great beauty. And yet in the world of women, there can be so much pain around our looks. The unwillingness to accept one's beauty, the insistence that certain flaws keep us out of the land of the beautiful, is a constant affirmation of not being enough, sufficient, whole in oneself. It's not like saying, "I'm not good at soccer." It's more like saying, "I don't belong," "I am not worthy."

By continuing to exclude ourselves, we misunderstand the nature and purpose of beauty. It is not a judgment or evaluation one person confers on another. Others can always change their minds. The courage to be beautiful is the courage to be alive, the courage to be filled with beauty.

The Perfection Merry-Go-Round

Often we are blocked from experiencing beauty by feelings of shame and ugliness. People moan about their short legs and their height, their teeth and their feet, their ugly elbows. We obsess about a million different things, fix on physical imperfections, compare the pain of being fat to acute illness. How do we meet this epidemic of self-hate, self-absorbed and painful at the same time, this desperate attempt to escape who we are?

Seeing our own beauty and ugliness asks us to draw on the qualities of compassion, gratitude, curiosity, discrimination, and acceptance. We need compassion to interrupt the mind's relentless self-criticism, gratitude for the body's many capacities, curiosity to go beyond our first perceptions. When we begin to see with acceptance, without the habitual filters of fear and judgment, many things we call ugly start to look different. When we begin to see past our images of beauty, there is more beauty around us than we ever imagined.

Listening to women describe other women they admire, the horse trainer who is skillful with children and animals, or the grandmother, round like dough, who bakes rolls at dawn and gives wonderful hugs, they comment, "She is not what people call beautiful, but she is beautiful to me." A therapist remembers, "There was a woman in the dressing room where I was swimming. She must have been eighty. And she was completely beautiful. She stood there naked, wrinkled, varicose veins, cellulite, scars, droopy skin—all the things old people have, the way we are when we're old. Things droop, things hang, legs, butt, belly. She wasn't particularly heavy, but she was quite old and she limped. She had this great radiance about her. We walked out of the dressing room with our clothes on. An elderly gentleman came to meet her. Both wearing white sneakers, white hair, she leaned on him because she's limping. They kissed in the sweetest way, gentle, glad to see each other. There was something absolutely gorgeous about who she was, the sweetness and kindness that came from her."

It is enormously sad the way we confuse self-respect with conceit, envy with admiration, become close by complaining about our flaws, compare, compare, compare ourselves. It hurts to hear women say, half-jokingly, "I hate you. You have such beautiful straight hair" or "such beautiful curly hair." "You're so voluptuous." "You're so thin." "I wish I was petite like you." "I wish I were tall." "I wish I had more ethnic looks." "I wish I was golden." "I wish I had breasts like yours."

These self-deprecating comments are painful to the person saying them and painful for the person hearing them. Our experiences of seeing each other and ourselves are permeated with comparisons. It's like we are eating lunch at the Good, Better, Best Café. No one will ever be good enough.

The "makeover" introduced in *Mademoiselle* in 1936 and promoted through the twentieth century in "before and after" pictures has been taken to new extremes as TV show hosts line up several normal women before plastic surgeons rating them and evaluating them on the spot. Who is served by all this grading, the constant comparing to a standard that is less and less real? Four-year-olds at nursery school deciding to have beauty contests, nine-year-olds dieting, old women feeling invisible. How much of our advertising is based on our not liking ourselves? How much therapy is based on attempting to address and remedy this self-hate?

A nurse-practitioner intent on educating her clients about the beauty of their bodies only half-jokingly suggests we throw our cars at our TVs. She introduces herself, "Hi, my name is Sandra. I'm in recovery from the American advertising industry." She is reminding them that in an extroverted culture, the attention continually goes to finding beauty outside ourselves. A geographer points out how real the women are in a French cuisine magazine. I listen eagerly as friends return from other places reporting what they notice walking down the streets, in restaurants, in the center of town in Hawaii, Russia, England, Israel, Vietnam. More than anywhere else, American society is driven by this intense preoccupation with a certain range of appearance. Yes, all people are moved by beauty, but American society has a very particular perspective not shared by the rest of the world.

We are experiencing an epidemic of self-hate that we are exporting all over the world, a kind of poverty that carries more pain than we can admit. Newspaper headlines report, "Tsunami of eating disorders sweeps across Asia"; "Prosperity means more Chinese well-fed: panic time." The first story describes how the self-starvation syndrome has spread to women of all socioeconomic and ethnic backgrounds in Seoul, Hong Kong, and Singapore. "Cases also have been reported—though at much lower rates—in Taipei, Beijing, and Shanghai. Anorexia has even surfaced among the affluent elite in countries where hunger remains a problem, including the Philippines, India, and Pakistan." In the second story the Chinese complain: "We're nearly as fat as the Americans." As workouts and diets cross cultures, the Chinese, who have been "cursed for centuries by famine," are now struggling with obesity.

Back in the United States, Christian diet books such as *More of*

Jesus, Less of Me and exercise programs such as "Faithfully Fit" combine evangelical theory and psychology, often linking losing weight with gaining God's love. Although we complain about the emphasis on thinness and obsession with weight, we accept that it is normal for women to spend more time worrying about food than enjoying it.

Even as we discuss these standards rationally, they get under our skin. We regard the designated beautiful people with envy and contempt and insist that they are shallow. We think their beauty makes their lives easy, invulnerable. James Wolcott points out how the supermarket tabloids delight in dissing celebrities, detailing weight fluctuations and singling out actresses who have the "bad taste to age ungracefully" by juxtaposing photos of them as young and radiant next to pictures of them in decline. It seems that there is no end to the perfection merry-go-round.

Within many families, the sisters, in twos and threes and fours, split the assignments. This one is pretty and that one is smart. This one is athletic and that one is brainy. Who gets to be whole? Who gets to be who she is? A story I heard about two girls, one studious and smart, the other more of a popular, pretty girl, illustrates the dilemma. Every year at Christmas, their parents would give the "smart" girl educational toys and books; the other daughter was given something more "frivolous." One year the cards on the presents were mixed up. Both girls were thrilled to be seen outside their assigned role.

Envy is one of the most insidious emotions, painful both for the one who experiences it and the one it is directed toward. It carries a feeling of being deeply uncomfortable when someone else shines; it brings with it a kind of loneliness that keeps us even more separate.

I have learned not to underestimate how deeply the comparing goes and how subtle and damaging it can be. Writing in *Yoga Journal*, poet and performance artist Blake More describes participating in a yoga teacher training in which everyone struggled with body image issues and diet. Unattainable images of physical perfection haunt many students. "For many of us with body-image issues, these ideals prove to us that, despite our daily practice, our bodies (and thus, we ourselves) are still not good enough. Far from being a sanctuary from our insecurities, yoga—and the yoga community—can reinforce them."

More charts her own journey: the slow process of moving away from the embattled gym mentality, the disillusion that comes as she confirms the eating disorder of one of her teachers when she bumps into her at the grocery store. She begins a program of self-study. Committed to experiencing her body from inside, she eliminates mirrors. She begins to practice in the nude, so her self-image is less influenced by the fit of her clothes. She moves with more acceptance through her monthly changes. With no mirror or teacher to correct her, she has no choice but to focus on her own experience, get inside her own skin. "Every time I practiced, it felt like I was rewiring the tracks of my awareness. The old tracks ran over every inch and bulge—complete with nasty comments pointing out my flaws and telling me I was a disgusting, fat, inflexible beast. The fresh ones didn't care about any of that craziness; they were laid down to help me negotiate peace inside the war zone of my body.

"And as these reparations unfolded, I found

that my 'hate tracks' were actually a blessing in disguise. Hate had helped me develop an intimate knowledge of my body—a knowledge that, through the practice of yoga, begged to be translated into love. Every posture became an opportunity to place a new awareness on an old message: I could now consciously choose whether I mapped my body with disgust or compassion. As positive choices became second nature, my self-criticism dropped away, leaving me open to other, more expansive energies."

As More demonstrates, it takes a fierce and tender compassion to stand up to the feelings of failure and futility that all too often spiral into active self-disrespect, self-forgetting, self-destruction. We need discipline to interrupt the drama in which we constantly evaluate our bodies and body parts as good and bad. It helps to recognize the interrelationship between envy and self-criticism, how both are amplified by the habit of constant comparison. Our contemporary American insistence on "improvement" is fueled by comparisons. We need to examine the images and see what we are being sold. And more and more, I believe it helps us to remember the beauty of the world that we are part of.

On a practical level, the greatest antidote to envy is gratitude. A woman who has put in many long hours in hospitals as a cardiac nurse notes, "Especially when I am able to do something, make something, or I take a walk in a beautiful place, I am so appreciative of the work my body does, what it gives me. It's easy to take this body for granted but it makes so much possible. I feel like a little kid whispering 'Thank you.' When I take a hike, I say, 'Thank you, feet, for walking with me to this place. Thank you, eyes, for seeing this landscape.' I feel so grateful to my body for taking me to the trees." Perhaps it's her occupational familiarity with death that makes her gratitude both credible and comforting.

Dilemmas and issues around our appearance may sound trivial, but they can become major features of the emotional landscape, linked to larger questions of identity, power, presence, perception, and soul. We forget that how we look to others and ourselves is influenced by how we feel. A woman confides that when she is feeling good in her relationship with her husband, she looks in the mirror and accepts what she sees. When their connection is more troubled, she looks in the mirror and sees "about twenty-five areas which could use plastic surgery."

As many of us are exiled from our own physical knowing and feeling, our own coherence and substantiality, we become more vulnerable and receptive to the media's images and definitions. We may complain about advertising, but we don't bring it to consciousness, we don't see what it means and how it lives in our bodies. Sculptor Kerry Vander Meer reclaims the materials of feminine experience, like cold cream and stockings, as media for her art. Reflecting on the moisturizer women apply in the morning, she started imagining how thick it would be over a lifetime. In her resulting sculpture *Skin Suit*, Vander Meer took cosmetics ads from magazines, embedding them in a cast-rubber body. The sculpture itself was part of an installation entitled *Ultimately Perfect*.

As we notice our hunger to improve ourselves, as if to prove we are worthy, we can stop and ask: Where in the body do these feelings live? Listen to the face, the heart, the skin, the muscles, the sexual organs. Sometimes we hear the criticism with which we paralyze ourselves, sometimes we hear the power and beauty of the life force. The loss of our energy and creativity in self-loathing is both wasteful and very sad. In the popular vernacular we talk about "self-trashing"—what a phrase, comparing ourselves to garbage! In the world of judgment and wanting things to be perfect, it can be very frightening to be oneself.

We, especially women, are trained early to measure our effects on others. We need to come back to ourselves and observe and inquire, investigate, witness: What is beautiful to us? What is pleasing? Where did I learn this self-hate? How do I transform the negativity and restore my energy and power? How do I participate in this beauty? Enjoying the act of embellishment is very different from feeling compelled to change one's appearance, or feeling that one is unacceptable, or hating one's looks.

One of the most radical things we can do is to stop despising and denying our physical shapes and forms. As much as we are frightened of ugliness, we are also terrified of our radiance. What does it mean to accept

and appreciate our looks, our faces and bodies, when we are ill, as we age? Are we able to cultivate a relationship with ourselves claiming what we know from the inside? Although it may seem self-centered, it is much less selfish than the obsessive preoccupation with our flaws.

What do we know in our core about the relationship between the inner self and the outer form? What do we want to present; what do we want to reveal? There is a confusion and frustration when we glimpse another way of being, of stepping out of the usual way of seeing and being seen, this deep hunger to be witnessed, perceived, and accepted. It can be very awkward to move between seeing with the eye of judgment and the eye of the heart, half caught in an old way of being and yet sensing, even remembering, that a larger and more generous vision is possible.

Reclaiming Beauty & Ugliness

Whole therapeutic industries are working to help people who have lost themselves to obsessions regarding body images and body parts. Whether it's someone who runs red lights because she doesn't want people staring at her while she's stopped, or someone who dances on a slippery floor with socks on because she's ashamed of her feet, the sufferers of body dysmorphic disorder are afraid people will regard them with loathing and disgust. Brown University psychiatrists found that, while women are more dissatisfied with their appearance, men and women suffer nearly equally from body dysmorphic disorder. The two major areas of obsession for men were body build and hair loss. This syndrome, in which sufferers are obsessed with imagined flaws in appearance, seems like a mad exaggeration of all the advertising we have ever seen. Shyness, embarrassment, shame, rage, many kinds of self-consciousness feed into this obsessive loathing.

At the psychology library at UC Berkeley, I hunt for references to beauty. The key words are "physical attractiveness," as if beauty were a simple set of ratios, proportions. In these scientific studies I sense an attempt to rationalize beauty's power to attract and to charm. Physical attractiveness lends itself to measurement and data analysis. The popular press brings us frequent excerpts: "Cute babies get more hugs," "Bosses won't hate you because you're beautiful," "If the choice is between getting plastic surgery or going to college, by all means go to college," "People who are attractive heal from back pain more quickly." In the past decade the number of studies has increased tenfold. Even though we are busy studying physical attractiveness, it still seems like we are missing something essential. The psychological studies feel unsatisfactory and incomplete because they don't acknowledge the generosity and diversity of the beauty of the life stream. They emphasize beauty as a survival value, focusing on the intersection between looks and health.

In his critique of evolutionary biology and "the new sciences of human nature," Louis Menand writes, "An obsession with the mean point of the bell curve has sometimes led scientists to forget that the 'average person' is a mathematical construct, corresponding to no actual human being. It represents, in many cases, a kind of lowest common denominator." He notes that in a recent experiment in which the ideal female face is constructed by blending all the features identified by people as most beautiful, the bland image that results is "far less alluring than many of the 'outlying' variants used to derive it." The focus in evolutionary biology on beauty as a signal of health, vigor, and fertility fails to take into account that humans find variations from the ideal attractive; our restless minds develop all kinds of capacities that aren't biologically essential.

Yes, we are attracted to beauty, but attraction brings beauty with it. Attractiveness is a good name for the biological spark, the excitement, the glimmer and hint, the play and possibility. Attraction pulls us closer together, closer to life, promotes the continuation of the species. We are social animals; we attract mates, friends; a woman attracts other members of her community to help raise her children. Attractiveness can be used to arouse desire, to advertise our availability, to motivate us, to delight and inspire us. Charmed and fascinated, we are drawn together.

By equating beauty with physical attractiveness, we continually try to make beauty a quality we can measure, evaluate, standardize, demystify, control, and explain. Attractiveness has a biological purpose, an evolutionary intention, a direction, an urgency. Beauty doesn't have any intention except to give and share joy. Attraction is active and insistent. Beauty allows us to rest. Beauty invites us to respond with our own beauty. Beauty speaks of our real connection to existence, beyond the mechanics and magic of attraction. Beauty is not simply a set of measurements, a shape, but the radiance and energy of the soul moving through the being.

A Ugandan cab driver in Seattle told me that there were fifty-two separate languages in Uganda; in his language, the word for "beauty" had different prefixes depending on whether you were referring to a beautiful person, tree, or car. We use the same word to describe a sexy body, computer software, wind in the trees, a series of photographs, the divine spark of radiance. No wonder we get confused and have to approach beauty sideways!

Etymologically, beauty is related to the Latin *bellus*, to *bonus*, to *beatitude*, *blessed*, and *good*. Beauty is a blessing, a gift from the senses to the soul. Beauty gives pleasure to the senses and exalts the mind and spirit. Awe, harmony, nobility are as much synonyms for beauty as comeliness and fairness. I like to think of the quality of beauty among other qualities. Beauty knows innocence and wisdom, harmony and power, intensity, radiance and coherence. Beauty is natural, exciting, and basic to life. Beauty, like pleasure, is wild and sweet. Sometimes beauty is outrageous and audacious and intricate, sometimes quiet, simple, austere. The beauty of the natural world is incredibly generous and abundant. Beauty is not simply perfection but wholeness, present throughout the life cycle of plants and animals. Looking at poppies, it is easy to see that the bud and the full bloom and the dying flower each reveal a different face of beauty. Our faces, like flowers, are beautiful across time.

We are starved for beauty, but in our hunger we keep thinking of beauty as something we can obtain, contain, possess, rather than as an essence that is always present. Stories like "The Ugly Duckling" and "Beauty and the Beast," in which surface ugliness gives way to a deeper beauty, endure because we long for our essential beauty to be seen and recognized. In these stories beauty becomes evidence of a way of life, rather than something to be strived for. Beauty includes the ability to change, to blossom, to let the spirit shine through, to keep present at each step.

"Beauty comes from seeing the world without the filter of fear. Ugliness is seeing the world through the filter of fear," a male therapist who works with disturbed teenagers notes. Beauty then becomes an act of courage, a willingness to see and be seen, a willingness to step forward, an act of honesty.

When I investigate what ugliness looks like and feels like, it seems that the hunger in ugliness is astonishing. The loneliness, too. The loneliness can never be filled; it is a loneliness for one's essential self and the angels, for trees and texture, for a deep sense of belonging. Looking up *ugliness* in the dictionary, the synonyms are charged with negativity and power: "Frightful, dire, hideous, offensive to the sight." We reject what we call ugly physically. Additional definitions for ugly include: "morally offensive, repulsive, troublesome, threatening, surly, quarrelsome."

There is a groan at the beginning of ugly. The ugggh of ugliness expressing everything from disgust to disdain to intensity. *Ugliness* is derived from the old Norse verb for "fear," clearly a clue. Many of us are afraid of ugliness, afraid of our own ugliness. Afraid to admit our own beauty, afraid that others will see our ugliness, we walk a jagged line between wanting to be seen for who we are and being afraid that who we are is not good enough. Perhaps the opposite of beauty is not ugliness but fear and apathy—fear that promotes uniformity; fear that envies boldness, audacity, and liveliness.

The suffering that ugliness makes us confront is powerful and mysterious. The Japanese word for "ugly" is literally written from characters that mean "painful to look at." The word denotes unbecoming, shabby, worn out, dishonorable, and by extension poor, bad, awkward. Many of the people and environments we label "ugly" confront us with suffering we would rather not see. It takes great compassion simply to look at something that is painful to see, to look at the parts of ourselves we call ugly.

Much of what is regarded as ugly is strong. A gardener points out that much of what we call ugly is chaotic, threatening, unpredictable, hairy, dark, animal, odorous. She says, "I am a messy person. I am not afraid to get my hands dirty." Because she has had her hands in the dirt for many years, she knows that ugliness is full of textures—scaly, leathery, wrinkled, slimy, gnarled, sharp, edgy. Associating ugliness with textures intrigues me because so much of what feels ugly about contemporary life is the flatness of textures and the anesthetizing of our senses in the built environment. We travel through the landscape in little steel capsules without seeing where we are going or feeling the way the air changes, pushed further and further away from natural rhythms.

When my students have written or spoken about what is beautiful and ugly in themselves and the world, there is so much ache and longing. Often people joke there is nothing beautiful about themselves, or renounce their beauty, proclaiming: "I am a member of the Ugly Club." In many situations, to admit one's beauty is to be vulnerable, to identify with ugliness is to be tough.

It is common for kids to describe beauty as clean, ugly as messy and disgusting. I'm curious about the balance between order and disorder, an order that is dynamic. Sometimes in the chaos and mess we find strength and beauty, variety and interest. The butterfly gardeners tell us if we want to bring back butterflies we have to stop manicuring our yards so much and learn to tolerate clutter. "Ecosystems, which someone's back yard can become, are complicated balances of nature. You can have a sterile, static, monochromatic garden with lawn and a few evergreen shrubs that take chemical fertilizers and water and pesticides to keep going. Or you can have a true ecosystem. Nobody takes care of a beautiful meadow in the Sierra."

Ugliness startles us and interrupts our attempts at perfection. Ugliness wears the mask of the adolescent girl and of midlife dread. Ugliness bites her nails, scratches her scalp, picks at her face, spits at mirrors, hides in plain sight, longs to speak, disrupts our attempts at perfection. Ugliness is a thief trying to steal our sense of belonging. Ugliness can also be very interesting, subtle, and lively.

The performer David Roche makes explicit our fear of ugliness in his one-man show, *The Church of 80% Sincerity*. Born with a face disfigured by a benign tumor, the skin on the left side has been burned purple by postsurgical radiation, and his pronunciation has been influenced by the loss of part of his mouth. When Roche begins to perform, he challenges the audience to see his face, to see him. "We with facial deformities are children of the dark," he announces. "Our shadow is on the *outside*. And we can see in the dark: we can see you, we see you turn away, but one day we finally understand that you turn away not from *our* faces but from your own fears. From those things inside you that you think mark you as someone unlovable to your family, and society, and even to God.

"All those years, I kept my bad stories in the dark, but not anymore. Now I am stepping out into the light. And this face has turned out to be an elaborately disguised gift from God." By the time his show is over, most people have stopped focusing on David's face because he has allowed them to see so much of his heart ... and themselves. He notes, "When I began to perform, I wanted to entertain. I thought about being humorous. I didn't realize I am stirring up deep unconscious memories of the times when people who were unacceptable were either killed or left to die." Early on, a woman came up to him after his show offering empathy and talking about the pain of her freckles. Roche incorporates this experience into his show as he describes his first impulse of ridicule for her story, the audacity of comparing the pain of freckles to facial disfigurement. Underneath he recognized the commonality of their suffering.

"People get a half-dozen quantum leaps from this hideous symbol. I'm OK and there's hope for them. At the core my work comes to grips with our perception of ourselves as ugly, useless, unattractive. That's the core part of spiritual emotional growth. All cultures are replete with shame." Roche reminds us that we have the capacity to see every person as ugly or beautiful, that the whole question of appearance disappears when we are completely engaged, when we stop seeing the form and see the person.

Ugliness is an important part of modern experiments with beauty because it shocks us, disturbs us, shakes us out of our complacency, makes us realize we are not in control. Ugliness, as much as beauty, stirs the emotions. Ugliness, like beauty, is a great teacher. Ugliness, perhaps even more than beauty, is in the eye of the beholder.

An art teacher instructs his adult students to make an ugly painting, and notes that people often reach for colors that they don't like. The works they bring to the wall at the end of the day are usually rough, the treatment coarse, energetic. He notices that the ugly pictures are never ugly the way we dread they will be. Often they evoke more visceral responses—not surprising given that they come from such a deep place in the self. He says, "In an art project what defeats the sense of ugliness is engagement." Free from trying to please, to control the outcome, to make something good or valuable, the artist makes something powerful. He adds, "When something is excessively beautiful, sometimes it is too precious. I feel betrayed by it. I want to have fluency with the qualities of beauty and ugliness and not be possessed by either."

A high school teacher intent on busting up her students' assumptions asks them to find something that is ugly in the beautiful and something beautiful in the ugly. It is an interesting assignment because it summarizes much of the energy and power of the art movements from the early twentieth century into our time. Artists often find ugliness interesting, or find what other people consider ugly to be full of creativity and reality. There certainly can be beauty in ruins, in what has been abandoned, discarded, worn out, marked by life. In a culture with so much emphasis on the new and the young, it makes sense that artists are attracted to the weathered and layered things, invite us to notice the surfaces we usually overlook, and find inspiration in the junk heap and the salvage yard as well as in prettier landscapes.

It sometimes seems that beauty has been exiled from the arts, especially the visual arts, but that is only partly true. In the drive to make works that are powerful and truthful, in a time when the "beauty of pretty" is so easily taken for advertising, in a time of nonstop war and ecological destruction, many artists have felt they must confront and challenge complacency. And as art has become more specialized and separate from people's lives, some artists have depended on more extreme images (and behavior) to challenge us and command our attention. Too many novels and movies give us myths of the crazy artist, the "meteors" whom the rest of society regards with a mixture of envy and contempt. These images of the artists' wildness emphasize a kind of narcissistic freedom but don't inform us how creative freedom is rooted in courage and discipline built over many years of trying, failing, trying again; how creativity is nourished by compassion and love as well as by outrage and angst.

At an art symposium, a speaker tells a roomful of artists and educators that artists are the people who break the rules. And a part of me thinks, *What rules, who makes up the rules?* and part of me thinks, *Yes, that is true*; sometimes, at certain points in history, artists have broken through the confinement of a conventional way of seeing the world and startled us with what they brought back. Artist as rebel, I know the archetype and the impulse. It is a heavy burden to carry full-time, a tremendous pressure to be original, to define oneself by "going against."

But one could also say artists cook up the culture. Sometimes artists break the rules, sometimes artists bring new eyes and hands to a tradition that is centuries old. Artist as researcher, traveler, translator, as witness and weaver, as, in Jerome Rothenberg's beautiful phrase, "technician of the sacred." In a culture with little memory, the artist is one who remembers. Artist as messenger, traveling between the past and the future, the handmade and the electronic, confirming humanity, affirming life, giving voice to what we know but cannot say. Artist as gardener, tending the soil, growing herbs and vegetables and flowers and soul.

"It's unfair to rupture and bring forth a wound without, at the same time, offering some solace. Not a cure-all, but a sense that there is something else that can be done," writes playwright Ntozake Shange. Many, many artists quietly working have found ways to offer solace, to look at what is difficult to look at and to celebrate the wounded heart, making work that is not afraid of beauty or ugliness, that honors suffering and also sings with joy.

I am inspired by artists who are neither breaking the rules for the sake of breaking the rules nor following the rules blindly. I love to listen to people who have spent a lifetime in the arts talk about being makers— the gratitude and generosity that comes from that making, the awareness of art as an offering. As Paulus Berensohn, master potter, dancer, weaver, and teacher, says, "We need not just art but the capacity to behave artistically."

I wonder how the freedom that artists achieve when they allow themselves to explore things we call ugly can be translated from art into other realms. I want to be able to discern between an ugliness that shuts us down and one that wakes us up, to see past my fears and also to speak out about the things that do seem spirit-killing. Learning to discern the ugliness that dulls the senses, numbs the soul, and cripples the life force is as much a challenge as learning to recognize true beauty.

The Riddles of Beauty
& Ugliness

In her beautiful meditation *The Work of Craft*, the potter Carla Needleman writes: "The beauty of the object derives from the quality of the work that went into it, from the attention that went into it. Technique doesn't play as big a part as we credit it with ... Quality of work is a difficult concept for us to understand. I realized that for the first time when I saw a broken and glued-together Chinese bowl offered at a high price. I cared, with my Western mentality, much more that it was broken than that it was beautiful. I wanted the object—intact—the integrity of the production was not something I could relate to." Carla Needleman is talking about a broken bowl, but the same attitude is evident toward the vessel that is the body. We are also patched and glued together, mended so that sometimes the edges show, sometimes the scars are well hidden. Well used, we are made beautiful by the way that we have lived.

Sometimes beauty is not revealed until we are broken open so the beauty can come through from the inside. A woman recalls, "I was the stereotyped Southern California teenager, long-legged, tall, slim, waist-length blond hair. When I gave birth at eighteen, the stretch marks were unbelievable. Stretch marks became my greatest teacher. I could easily have lived a vapid lifestyle, but these huge red lines made me look underneath the surface, review my concept of perfection." Broken so the beauty comes forward, our brokenness is not a flaw to be covered up but an opportunity for the beauty inside to become more apparent.

Similarly, the Japanese aesthetic of *wabi-sabi* celebrates the humble, irregular, and impermanent. According to designer Leonard Koren, who has spent much of his adult life in Japan, "Wabi-sabi is ambivalent about separating beauty from nonbeauty or ugliness. The beauty of wabi-sabi is, in one respect, the condition of coming to terms with what you consider ugly."

Wabi-sabi asks us to look into and beyond the pretty surface of things. Koren writes, "To the wealthy merchants, samurai, and aristocrats who practiced tea [ceremony], a medieval Japanese farmer's hut, which the wabi-sabi tearoom was modeled on, was quite a lowly and miserable environment. Yet, in the proper context, with some perceptual guidance, it took on exceptional beauty. Similarly, early wabi-sabi tea utensils were rough, flawed, and of undistinguished muddy colors. To people accustomed to the Chinese standards of refined, gorgeous, and perfect beauty, they were initially perceived as ugly. It is almost as if the pioneers of wabi-sabi intentionally looked for such examples of the conventionally nonbeautiful—homely but not excessively grotesque—and created challenging situations where they would be transformed into their opposite."

Like wabi-sabi, the French expression *jolie-laide* calls our attention to less obvious and refined beauty. Jolie-laide, literally meaning pretty/ugly, describes a person who is not conventionally thought of as beautiful or gorgeous but who is compellingly attractive. Writing about the great French fashion designer Coco Chanel, JoAnn Gitlin notes that Chanel was the classic example of the jolie-laide, adding, "Even a homely Frenchwoman can make a pretty American look as bland as a Barbie."

Both wabi-sabi and jolie-laide allow ugliness and beauty to coexist; they hint at the elusive, unpredictable, and paradoxical nature of beauty.

Often what we think of as beautiful is defined by its not being ugly. When we dismiss something as ugly, we become unable to find beauty in it. By focusing so much on the immediate appearances, we continually forget how much we need to make ourselves available to receive beauty. As wabi-sabi shows us, Koren says, "Beauty can spontaneously occur at any moment given the proper circumstances, context, or point of view. Beauty is thus an altered state of consciousness, an extraordinary moment of poetry and grace."

What I like about wabi-sabi and jolie-laide is how these concepts bring beauty back into some other realm. It is not only a matter of form and appearance, it is an invitation to engage with form and appearance, to take into account intention and feeling, to go past our familiar perceptions. Beauty comes to us through our senses, but there is also an aspect of beauty that is invisible, or is not perceived by the senses, or that comes through the senses and takes us somewhere else.

There is a way in which beauty and ugliness are opposites and are something we recognize intuitively, viscerally, and there is also a way in which beauty and ugliness are neighbors, are adjacent to each other, borrow each other's clothes, take each other's parts in the play. There is a way in which beauty is obvious and radiant and generous. There are also beauties that are hidden and deep and mysterious. I experience many things as ugly. I am fussy and sensitive, and sometimes I don't like the texture of the sheets on the bed, the sound of the planes landing, the cheap construction of so many buildings. Yet I know enough to go past my first reactions; some things that seem ugly are powerful or difficult, unfamiliar or interesting. Sometimes it is important to protest against ugliness and sometimes it is important to go beyond our beliefs and judgments. The twilight places where ugliness and beauty coexist are full of interest and surprise.

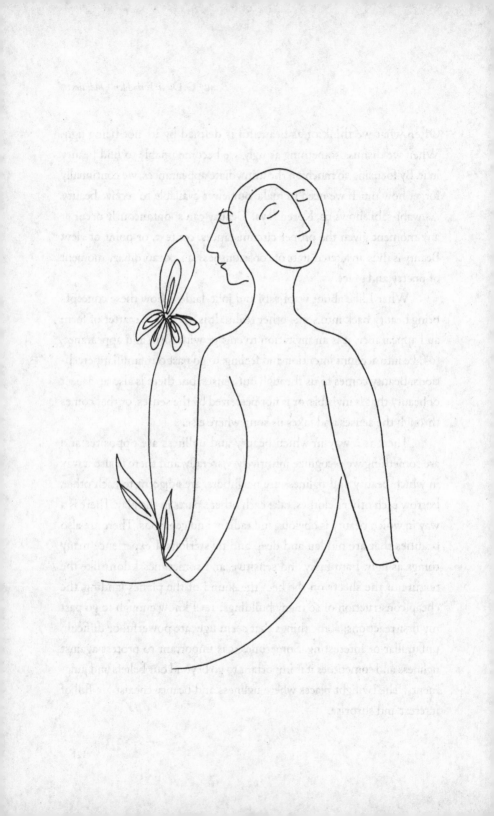

Faces & Masks

My face is like a museum where people go to look
at everything there.
They look at expressions and moods.
There's even a little restaurant on the first floor:
My mouth.
People take the nose elevator up to my eyes,
bouncing on my hair.
They practice Tarzan swinging by their ropes,
screaming in my ears.
At night
when I'm awake,
it's closing time.
Everything disappears into my head
until tomorrow.

Alexandra Dunn
fourth grade

An eighth grader asks, "If there weren't any mirrors, would we all think we are beautiful?" His teacher comments on how she looks better in some mirrors than in others. We may all be mirrors for each other, but we are not exact reflections, and sometimes we meet different selves in different faces, different selves in different mirrors. A woman notes that when her husband takes pictures of her she always looks pretty; when her mother photographs her, she looks terrible.

One of my dictionaries says, "The notion that a person's face 'is' their appearance, what they look like to the rest of the world, lies behind the word *face*." The original Latin, *facies*, meant "appearance" or "form," and eventually came to signify the face.

Does your face look like you? Sometimes a mirror is a useful tool in exploring that question; sometimes the mirror gets in the way. A baby looking in the mirror sees that self both as self and friend. When did we forget that? Unclothed, undecorated, naked, open: our faces take the slap not simply physically but verbally—meet bad words, judgments, uninvited sexual innuendo as well as air and light and love that shines in others' faces. In traditional beauty books, the reader is asked to stand in front of the mirror to assess and evaluate the strengths and weakness of her face; frequently, in the name of evaluating our appearances, we catalogue our flaws. How we look is often how we are expected to look.

In the mirror's reflection sometimes we stare straight into the face of our culture—the expectations, shadows, fantasies, nightmares. In our faces we face the fear of aging. The structure of prejudice, its blatant stereotypes and insidious assumptions, is built from very specific descriptions of facial structures, noses, lips, and eyebrows, assigning personal characteristics to physical appearance. Much plastic surgery has been performed to minimize ethnic features, to make faces look more WASP.

Poet Alison Luterman articulates these expectations in a poem that describes how her grandmother comments on weight gain or loss, hair, and finally works up to the irresistible, forbidden topic: the nose. Offering to pay for a "nose job," her grandmother's fingers "dry as aristocrats, trace / on my stubborn resisting peasant's face / the outlines of a perfect potential nose." At the end of her poem, Luterman claims an older lineage:

The whole face is my gift,
this round, quizzical, and flyaway face,
attached to earth by way of pendulous breasts,
long waist, hips like sloping hills;
all, all verboten in my grandmother's eyes.
But what can I do?
I have another Grandmother, eons older,
she of the scales and feathers, she of the fur;
goddess of hoof, horn, beak and claw.
Gnarled and riven, wiser than fashion by far.
She decreed my beauty hers
long ago and even condemned me to praise
it endlessly. I stand on my nose.

For all the faddishness of "ethnicity" in the fashion world, our beauty standard has been geared toward the ordinary, the mainstream, the cute, the dominant culture of the conquerors. How many mothers, knowing the pain of marginalization, try to tame, to tone down, to enforce the mainstream standards, straightening their daughters' frizzy hair, controlling their calories, trying to shape their girl children's faces and bodies into a more acceptable appearance. Certainly fathers, boyfriends, siblings add to the chorus, but most often the mothers are the agents and arbiters, passing on their own beliefs and wounds in the attempt to protect their offspring.

Social historian Kathy Peiss notes that "cosmetics and paints marked distinctions between and within social classes; they also reinforced a noxious racial aesthetic. Nineteenth-century travelers, missionaries, anthropologists, and scientists habitually viewed beauty as a function of race. Some writers found ugliness in the foreign born, especially German,

Irish, and Jewish immigrants." Nowadays such nonsense is no longer pronounced blatantly by scientists and anthropologists, but the lingering assumptions of the superiority of white beauty are subtly reinforced in the numerous images that surround us.

"Discrimination is not just shouting insults, or jobs," writes Asian American poet David Mura, "it's how you react emotionally when you see a face: Are you curious about that face? Do you feel affectionate towards that face? Do you feel a desire to understand and to know what's going on in that person's interior life? Does that

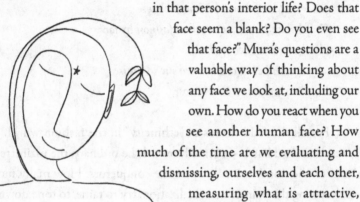

face seem a blank? Do you even see that face?" Mura's questions are a valuable way of thinking about any face we look at, including our own. How do you react when you see another human face? How much of the time are we evaluating and dismissing, ourselves and each other, measuring what is attractive, what is acceptable, worthy?

The deluge of faces we have been exposed to, the close-ups of faces in movies, in magazines, billboards, are a recent part of human consciousness of self and other. In our narcissistic culture, we take this increased attention to presentation for granted, but there have been many times and places where images and reflections were scarce. Who can say how we would feel about ourselves, our bodies, our faces, each other, if we grew up in a world without the feedback of mirrors, the instructions of photographs, the constant company of perfect strangers in our media. Would our dreams be different, the way we use our eye muscles, the way we kiss?

What is it to look at a face, not to immediately grade, judge, reject, but to look and look? What is it to look at our own faces as well as others with affection, curiosity, respect? A woman tapes up pictures of herself as a young girl around her bedroom. For months, when she sees these pictures, she sees herself as hideous. One day she is able to look at the photos and see her own sweetness. We insist that we are seeing clearly, even when it is clear we have many filters that keep us from seeing our beauty.

An exercise in *Drawing on the Right Side of the Brain* instructs the reader to take a high-contrast black-and-white photo of a face, turn it upside down and draw it, turn it right side up and draw it again. The upside-down drawings are often more true, more accurate, even if the lines are more awkward because the artist has stopped knowing what a face is as she draws its suddenly unfamiliar shape. I wish we could do this with our own faces, and see them anew.

From infancy we are engaged and fascinated by the human face, the faces of those we love. Research psychologist Alison Gopnik says that even forty-five-minute-old newborns imitate the facial expressions of others. When the experimenter sticks out his or her tongue, alert babies stick out their tongues in imitation. "What that means is that there is a deep link from the time you are born between your internal body states and feelings—that very personal sense of how you are—and what you see when you see other people, when you see a face and a body." Infants pay special attention to faces, she suggests. "And by the time they are three or four months old they are engaged in a kind of rhythmic byplay. The best description of it is flirtation; three- and four-month-old babies are always flirting with the people around them."

I had wanted to write that the human face is one of the most interesting and beautiful things of all, the way anything resembling a face
catches an infant's attention, the way even after a century of abstract art,
portraiture remains compelling. But I'm stumbling over the word *thing*.
What is the face? The face, like the soul, can never be a thing. The face
is a direction, a dimension; perhaps, the face is the shape of the soul.
Perhaps we have made a mistake calling the face a noun because it is
always moving, always changing, always *facing*, animated by expression
and breath and light.

The face is a location, an event, a directory, a map. The heart's
suburbs. The city's limits. The face is a history book. We love to see the
old man in the baby's face, the boy looking out from the old man's eyes.
A *New Yorker* cartoon shows a woman leaving after plastic surgery with
her old face in a bag. The woman who cuts my hair imagines writing a
science fiction story set in Southern California in the next century. A man
and a woman are married. When they have their first child, the child is a
revelation. They had both had so much plastic surgery that neither knew
what the other truly looked like until they saw their child.

The face is etched with emotion, the face is edged with shadow. The
face speaks of mind and heart, self and soul, ancestors and descendants.
Photographers and makeup artists remember what we sometimes forget:
the face is outlined, clarified, defined by light.

"Every face is like a new irregular past-tense verb," says a man as he
struggles to learn Spanish at midlife. Given how many faces there are in
our lives, it is remarkable how instantly we recognize the faces that belong
to people we know. The brain recognizes patterns, regions, provinces of
the face rather than simple features.

"The face is what I connect with to make the world real," says my
friend Lynne Williams, who has owned a facial salon for twenty years,

who has touched many people's faces with her healing hands. "I look around the room and look for the face that looks back at me. It's not that it is a face as much as it's a heart. It's a circle, from your face to that other face."

When you're beginning to love someone, you see his or her face reflected everywhere. And yet at times it is hard to remember the faces of those we love most. When the face of someone close becomes angry or pained, we are shocked that the one who seemed so loving or wise or kind turns into a harsh and self-absorbed stranger. A woman says her husband doesn't like the way she looks when she's angry. And when she is upset with him, she believes his face gets longer, his chin more pointed, his nose looks "thin."

Another woman remembers how, when she was a girl, she would see her mother look in the mirror and say, "I don't look like that," and she would say, "You do, Ma. Yes, you do." Now she looks in the mirror and thinks, "I don't look like that." In her mid-eighties, my great-aunt said, "I feel like a young girl, but I have the face of an old woman."

The most precious faces are the ones we can't practice in the mirror. The face of a person broken open in grief, the faces of love. In its most vulnerable moments, the face becomes its own being. One of the possible etymologies for *face* connects with the word *fax*, torch. Our faces give off light; sometimes our faces become lanterns that can light the way for others. A wise old man, close to death, looks into his young friend's loving face looking back at him and says, "I don't know who you are, but I love you."

I love the formal words for the face: *demeanor, countenance, visage, mien. Countenance* echoes with the memories of the prayer book: "May God's countenance shine upon you."

Our faces don't just belong to us. We give them to each other. Our faces may be more familiar to our loved ones than to ourselves. Even when we are listening, our faces are speaking. Looking out, the face is speaking; looking in and away and through, the face speaks not in discrete syllables but in expressions of surprise and wonder, rage and flashes of panic, anguish and awe, all kinds of intensities we don't announce or translate into words. As the silent-film actress Gloria Swanson said, "We didn't need dialogue. We had faces."

"My face is full of meanings and feelings," a fifth grader declares. We don't have much practice describing the phases and facets, the faces of a face. Perhaps that is why we have novelists and profile writers who paint a face with their words, imbuing their description of features with a description of character. Bill Buford writes: "I've been studying Lucinda Williams's face—a youthful face, soft skin, few wrinkles, a face so much younger-looking than her age that waspish peers whisper that she must have submitted it to the surgeon's nick and tuck. She hasn't. Its dominant quality is its changeableness. This is a face full of weather—or, maybe, more accurately, it's akin to a weather report, a forecast of the personality you're going to see next. Now, the two of us in her living room, in the evening . . . her face is relaxed and expressive, and yields easily to a teasing, cackling laugh—a laugh that makes you feel appreciated and enjoyed. In concert, she has another face, and one that rarely gives up so much as a smile. It firms up, reveals little, and is at odds with the expressive songs she sings."

"No poker face," my mother informed me when I was a teenager, bemoaning my vulnerability, relieved at my inability to lie. All our emotions show in our face. With forty-four muscles, a tremendous amount of motor activity is centered in the face. The muscles of the body are attached to our bones, but the muscles of the face are also attached to the skin, enabling our face to respond quickly to the brain's instructions.

As we may have heard in admonitions to be more cheerful, it takes more muscles to frown than to smile.

When elementary school students write about their faces, it is delicious to hear the brightness and audacity of their images: the face becomes a flower, a continent, a globe, a planet. In their writings, the face is curious, open, excited. A student writes, "My face is like a detective who wants to learn new things about what's going on." Another conveys her enthusiasm, "My face reminds me of firecrackers on the Fourth of July."

When does the exuberance of the young students' writings about their faces give way to the teenager's looking in the mirror, frowning at her face, viewing every pimple as a volcano, the vehement expressions of adolescent self-loathing? Is it possible to interrupt the self-conscious preoccupation with self-image that begins in adolescence and challenge the lack of generosity with which we often greet our own faces?

As the students search for metaphors and similes, we agree it may not be possible to say what a face is; maybe it's more effective to say what the face does. Several students travel through the landscape of the face. The face is a light source: flame, lamp, and star. The eyes are planets, the ears are ships sailing across the sea of the alphabet, the nose is a thief stealing scents. "My face is like a post office," a student tells us, describing the face as message central. The classroom becomes "a garden of faces."

Some faces are like sunflowers that reach toward the sunlight, some are quiet and mysterious, like rare blooms that blossom once a year in the middle of a warm night. The faces that children draw on the moon and the summer sun and on flowers insist that our world is full of faces; many things are looking at us.

Once I dreamed of all my books turning into flowers and as I woke up, I imagined each flower connected with a face. There was something wonderful about books being faces and flowers, faces being flowers and books, sources of beauty and wisdom. The faces of those we love are like books that we return to again and again—dictionaries, atlases, directories, songbooks. The face is one of my favorite texts. The face is one of my favorite flowers.

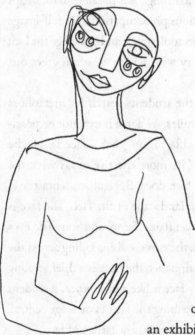

Putting on Your Face

*I use a different shade of lipstick
for every character I dance.*

Julie Kent
American Ballet Theatre ballerina

As certain makeup ads make clear, with their artfully arranged palettes of color and jars of brushes, the face is also a kind of canvas, a locus of self-creation. At an exhibit at the Museum of Modern Art in

New York several years ago I saw a "painting" made out of eye shadow boxes. Artist Rachel Lachowicz took the colors of the makeup counter as her media, constructing an abstract geometric painting out of small rectangles, alternating shades of violet, dusty rose, green, blue, gray, and bronze. Seeing all the luscious colors juxtaposed in neat rows, seeing the media of makeup become the media of art, emphasized how much decorating one's face is like making a painting.

Face painting has long been the territory of alchemists and chemists. Our word *cosmetic* is derived from the Greek word *kosmetikos*, which referred to the art of beautifying the body, to cultivating beauty over time as well as temporarily covering up blemishes and enhancing key features. The word *cosmos* refers to the order of the universe, and *cosmic* and *cosmetic* suggest a harmony between one's physical appearance and the order of the physical world.

Decorating the face has been a part of religion and ritual throughout the world. Makeup has not been limited to one sex or part of daily presentation but used to alter the face into something both more and less human. Warriors and priests in many traditional and tribal cultures have painted their faces with clay and natural pigments, adding elaborate headdresses with feathers, beads, flower petals, and other vegetation. Such face painting effectively transformed the face into a mask.

What does it mean to "put on a face"? How is wearing makeup different at thirteen, at thirty-five, at fifty-two? Women wear a face to a job, to dress up, for fun, to attract someone, to be part of a conversation between strangers adjusting their makeup in the mirrors. A contemporary designer who refers to her makeup as "war paint" notes, "After Queen Elizabeth cut off her hair and whitened her skin, she became a very successful leader; before she did that she was too vulnerable. I wear makeup because I have a very innocent face, and I want to be more powerful at work."

Modern makeup makes us both more visible and more invisible. We use makeup to enhance, to decorate and transform, to bring out a self that others don't usually see. We react to the falseness of it, enjoy the theater of it. Makeup carries multiple meanings in the course of a woman's life, sometimes within the course of a single day.

"I could commit a murder or rob a bank and no one would see me, I am so washed out without makeup. It's like I'm driving without a car," a woman notes, contrasting her pale Irish features with those of the tall Cuban women she used to go dancing with in her partying days. An acupuncturist remembers that years ago, when she tended bar, she noticed that when she wore makeup, she consistently made better tips. Although it has been reported that women who wear makeup make better salaries in the corporate world, she wonders if it was the makeup that people were reacting to or the change in herself. When she wore makeup, she approached the job more like she was playing a part.

My friend Valerie comes to California and complains how naked our faces look in Berkeley, the last bastion of naturalism, and advises me, long-distance, what color lipstick and eye shadow to wear with a wonderful new black dress for an important occasion. In the casual environment where I spend most of my time, I often feel conspicuous wearing makeup. I ask women who are self-employed if they wear jewelry when they are working by themselves, and mostly they say yes. Makeup when one's working at home? Mostly no, though I know a rural artist who carefully puts on her makeup and jewelry in the morning but doesn't always bother to wear any clothes.

A woman shares how she feels conspicuous without makeup. When she feels vulnerable in the world, she wears makeup as her mask, putting a layer of protection between herself and others. When she goes home and washes the makeup off, it signals that she is off-duty, she can be herself.

With the billions of dollars spent on beauty products that couldn't possibly do what they claim, the obsessive rituals and the artifice, makeup has many critics. A friend complains that, growing up in the New York suburbs, he developed an "aesthetic allergy" to bright fingernail polish. The sixteenth-century poet John Donne viewed women who painted themselves as "taking the pencil out of God's hand." In the eighteenth century, the English parliament passed laws that annulled the marriages of women who used scents, paints, artificial teeth and hair to attract a mate. Darwinians frowned on artificial enhancement because it interrupted the evolutionary process and interfered with men choosing the best mate. Women have been fired from jobs both for wearing too much makeup and for not wearing any makeup.

Along with women who have openly enjoyed makeup, other women proudly disassociated themselves from such artifice, whether it was nineteenth-century farm women, priding themselves on their simple routines, or the 1920s "soap and water women," to contemporary women alert to the $50 jar of cream containing $2 worth of ingredients, critical of the toxic ingredients and false health claims of cosmetics, and articulate about the hypnotic effects of advertising.

Historian Kathy Peiss has read the old beauty books, looked at the ad strategies of cosmetics companies in the twentieth century, examined the meaning of whitening the face with toxic paints in the white and black communities. She puts the consumer culture of cosmetics in a historical context, describing how the homemade complexion products of the nineteenth and early twentieth centuries evolved into the comprehensive systems of skin care that we have today. The beauty industry was one of the few places where women entrepreneurs thrived, and it was through the efforts of women such as Elizabeth Arden and Helena Rubenstein in the white community and Madam C. J. Walker and Annie Turbo Malone in the black community that skin care and makeup grew into a major industry. Peiss named her book on beauty culture *Hope in a Jar*, echoing Revlon founder Charles Revson's promise that makeup could transform one's life into something more glamorous; at times it seems it would be more accurate to call these skin-care products "despair in a jar."

The contradiction of using makeup as a symbol for women to explore and portray their individuality is not lost on contemporary women. We may critique the marketing of makeup at the same time that we take pleasure in the act of embellishment. We acknowledge the media's power to reflect and shape the way we regard ourselves and look at others, understand that we are paying too much for a moisturizer, and still enjoy buying a bright new lipstick.

As the founder of The Body Shop, the British-based cosmetics company, Anita Roddick has looked at the traditional methods of skin and hair care of women all over the world, seeking to document these recipes before they are lost. Roddick's humble beginnings, selling in a small shop in southern England, are reminiscent of an earlier era. By using refillable bottles, emphasizing education rather than false advertising, and offering a variety of ingredients from around the world, Roddick's company claims a business ethic that includes a commitment to international social justice and environmental issues. She identifies herself in the centuries-old tradition of the trader: "It is immoral to trade on fear. It is immoral constantly to make women feel dissatisfied with their bodies. It is immoral to deceive a customer by making miracle claims for a product. It is immoral to use a photograph of a glowing sixteen-year-old to sell a cream aimed at preventing wrinkles in a forty-year-old."

Roddick is one of the most visible spokeswomen, but even in the age of huge cosmetic companies, there are many independent entrepreneurs, "radical traditionalists" inspiring us to take care of ourselves and live healthfully, returning skin care and makeup to its roots as a shared culture between women. With more attention to high-quality ingredients and less focus on advertising, these companies appeal to our hunger for what's real and carefully made. As we become more alert to the importance of healthy food and more sustainable agricultural practices, this awareness extends to skin care and cosmetics; we want to choose products that are not harmful to ourselves or the environment.

There is also something empowering and nourishing about "kitchen cosmetics," making one's own products out of the ingredients at hand. Meeting with a new friend, we make oatmeal lavender soap, and I regard soap differently now that I have made some myself. Soap making, like making beer and bread, wine and cheese, is a craft that feels artistic, ancient, alchemical, as basic ingredients are cooked and transformed. So many kinds of soap: Mediterranean soaps based on olive oil and honey, jasmine soaps from China, Brazilian soaps made from honey that smell like caramelized sugar, the perfumed clays of the Middle East, the soapwort plant used by indigenous Americans and ancient Egyptians. It is beautiful that something as ordinary and essential as soap can be as wholesome as olive oil, as sweet as honey, as common as milk, as luxurious as the scents of sandalwood, vanilla, and roses.

We can cook up face masks and moisturizers like we're making cookies and cakes and fruit salads, using oatmeal, almond meal, cornmeal, egg whites, buttermilk, cream, and salt. Strawberries, cucumbers, mango, avocado, papaya, yogurt. The scents of herbs and flowers—roses, ginger, rosemary, lavender, marigolds—become sources of subtle intentions.

In contrast to skin-care and makeup products that are constantly advertised as new and improved, these basic recipes have been passed on for centuries, a legacy of beauty secrets that nourish the body and feed the senses. There is an ecological logic at work here. Olive oil, palm oil, coconut oil, sesame oil—local oils have long formed the base for the body oils of choice. Indian women use a ground turmeric powder to give their skin an amber glow; Japanese geisha dust their faces with rice powder. These rituals of care speak of the abundance of the kitchen and garden, the sense of community among women.

In *The Art of Imperfection* Veronique Vienne writes, "Probably the most effective beauty regimen is to get up in the morning and say, 'Wow.'" Artist Donna Henes takes this one step further when she notes that every time she looks in the mirror to apply her lipstick, she blesses her mouth, "what goes into and what comes out of it."

Sacred Masks, Inner Faces

Makeup is only one of the masks we wear. Often painted on by the culture, the face we need to keep up an appearance, "save face," the masks presented for women and men can be tight, uncomfortable, difficult to wear. But masks are not only false faces or simple disguises. Masks also serve as doorways to the spirit. Looking at contemporary and traditional masks, we learn about other peoples and cultures, appreciate the way art can be integrated into the political and spiritual life of a community.

Dramatizing the features of the face has long fascinated us—from the masked figures in the cave paintings at Lascaux to Picasso's bold portraits, which turn our features on their sides, inspired by the artist's affinity for African masks. Even in societies that no longer regard masks as sacred, we are intrigued by their power and mystery. Constructed from every kind of material, masks may be highly elaborate or very simple. Masked rituals marking birth, puberty, marriage, and death have been part of human culture for millennia. Masks are worn at harvest celebrations, funeral processions, festivals, and political occasions of all kinds. Humans have masked their faces in rituals to facilitate food gathering, hunting, and planting.

In Bali, hundreds of masks are used both in sacred temple dances and in performances for tourists. Certain basic archetypes are very common: the king, prime minister, queen. When I was visiting, I was intrigued by the relationship between the archetype and the object. The Balinese were not concerned that the tourists were corrupting their culture because they could offer the public one version of their culture and still keep their sacred traditions for themselves. For example, there is the mask of the prime minister carved by a respected artisan, the "museum-quality" mask of the prime minister bought by collectors, the cheap masks for tourists on Monkey Forest Road. These masks may all be the prime minister, but they differ not only in aesthetic quality but in intention. The ceremonial masks are carved by priests whose prayers inform every step of the mask-making—from choosing the wood from an appropriate tree to preparing the paints to painting the mask with a specified number of coats of paint.

These sacred masks are displayed only as part of the entertainment for the gods and goddesses during a temple festival.

For the Balinese, writes anthropologist Hildred Geertz, masks "may serve as lightning rods, to collect momentarily a portion of the cosmic energy, the vital life of the universe ... While present in this world, these energies have no material form in themselves and must take up residence in vessels provided them. And while here, they are entertained by feasting, music, and dance. Balinese today stress that their religion is monotheistic, but that their God takes as many forms as the sun has rays. Each time the divine force visits the world, it comes as clouds of beings of all shapes and potencies, and it comes in different places at the same time."

Masks remind us that theater has its roots in sacred ritual, and many theatrical traditions throughout the world employ masks in both traditional and innovative ways. Japanese Noh masks, carved from a piece of cypress wood, offer a neutral expression that seems to become animated by the skill of the actor. Some Kalabari masks are worn on the top of the head to face the sky, an impossible position for an actor to sustain.

The mask is an intersection of artifact and living body. It is both symbol and vehicle of transformation. The lines in the mask emphasize emotion; the planes of the mask reflect light, especially the highly polished Balinese and Noh masks. The mask meets the lines of the body in movement. The mask comes alive as it is worn and performed.

At a time when we are experiencing a renewed interest in the mythic, the shamanic, and the sacred, masks are showing up in a variety of ways and places. Twenty-five years ago, textile artist Maggie Sherman made plaster-tape face masks of more than four hundred of the six hundred residents in her hometown of Montgomery, Vermont, which each person then decorated themselves. Sherman's project in turn inspired the Oakland, California, arts fair, Festival at the Lake, to organize the project "1,000

Faces," emphasizing the diverse faces of Oakland residents, from well-known artists, athletes, musicians, and politicians to "ordinary" people.

Making masks with teenagers, I have experienced firsthand how much masks can serve as an affirmation of identity. Putting on and taking off masks is both playful and serious. It opens us up to other masks we have only dreamed about taking off, faces we've only dreamed about expressing. In making plaster-tape masks, we have the opportunity to experience the face under the mask, to go inside the face, and then, as the mask hardens on the face, to experience literally removing the mask. Looking at people's faces at these moments, glopped up with bits of plaster tape and Vaseline, tender and new, it is like we are molting and shedding old skins, we are butterflies emerging from the chrysalis; we are ancient actors at an initiation ceremony.

Watching as people first begin to paint masks, I am struck by how often we divide the face into two faces, often opposite, within the single face. Sometimes, as a warm-up exercise, I have asked people to make faces on two sides of a brown paper bag, a face they present to the world and a face that is more hidden, the face of an ancestor and a face from the future, writing poems and dialogues between the faces along the sides of the bag.

Masks are especially suited to metaphor, portraying essence, broadcasting an emphatic expression. The impersonality of the mask brings with it a safety that allows us to say things we can't say at other times. Behind the mask, we can practice and experiment with energy and movement, breath and voice, dimensions of ourselves that have not been visible. Taking the mask off, we greet our familiar face with respect and humor, tenderness and curiosity. So this is the face I have been given to wear, this is what remains constant, this is what constantly changes. Making these simple masks becomes a tangible expression of soul, an opportunity to inquire what parts of yourself yearn to become more visible.

What we casually dismiss as the false face of the mask may be the picture of a spirit, or an inner face, that we have yet to integrate. We struggle against the false faces of imposed roles, delight in the many changing faces of the self. Often when I make masks, I leave one eye open, one eye closed, one eye looking out to the world, one eye looking inside to the imagination, the back of the skull, the dark interior of the body. Through the years, as I have made dawn masks and night masks, a mask of the confused moon and the moon sister, the skeleton and the gypsy, Courage and Charm, I am reminded that each mask offers a different facet of the soul.

When I was involved in the staging of a play based on *The Book of Qualities*, we developed a scene with the characters of Fear, Terror, Panic, and Courage. As one dancer entered, he carried a large round brown mask of Courage on a stick, encircled by six face-size masks of Courage. The figures of Fear, Terror, and Panic were costumed in larger-than-life-size masks with exaggerated features. At various points in the scene, the actors each put on one of the small masks of Courage. The point was not simply to stage a battle in which Courage triumphed and Fear was forever vanquished, but to play with the combinations between Terror and Fear, Fear and Panic, Courage and Terror, Panic and

Courage, among many kinds of Courage. These exchanges suggested that we dance with Courage and then become Courage dancing, six of us dancing together, each carrying a different face of Courage: the courage to see, to love, to speak, to walk alone, to be our most beautiful, outrageous, courageous selves, the Courage that stands next to Terror, that eats breakfast with Panic, that works in the office next to Fear. Small everyday courage and capital C Courage. We are dancing between our courage and our terror, within ourselves, between ourselves, among ourselves. We keep changing places, exchanging faces. In some ways the masks were too fixed. It's not an accident that this masked dance was dedicated to courage and fear. Beneath the masks and in the looking glass and in the mirror of each other's faces, we find courage and fear, terror and beauty.

The questions "Who are you, what are you, where did you come from?" are among the great questions. The question "Who am I?" is asked in youth, asked in midlife, asked in anguish during sleepless nights, asked in wonder at moments when the heart breaks open to the truth. It is a question that lovers ask each other in wonder and terror and delight. It is a question that penetrates through layers of masks. It is a question that sometimes our faces can answer and sometimes asks our faces to dissolve. It is a wonderful question to ask and ask; in each asking, a different facet of the totality of what we are emerges.

"I am a feather on the bright sky," reports the Native American writer N. Scott Momaday. "I am an unskilled architect who's been asked to build a palace for the king," says Lalla, an Indian woman mystic six centuries ago. "I am the fifth season, the warmth in the fog," a contemporary high school girl writes.

Our answers are imaginative and ecological, connecting us with the local details of animal and plant life, extending us into the galaxies and through time. In their expansiveness they suggest how we can flow into many kinds of life. The question "Who am I?" invites us to reach into and out of ourselves, to discover the secret source of our beauty, to belong to the life stream. It loosens the masks we wear every day and unbinds the conviction with which we limit ourselves to our appearance. It suggests we are much more than we know. We both are and are not the faces and forms we wear.

What do you see when you look in the mirror? Does your face look like you? Who are you? The questions invite us to examine the relationship between the form the world sees and how we feel inside, the coherence underlying many expressions. We have the same face all our lives, and we have a different face every second. The face of the moment reveals the face of eternity. Each of our faces is a part of God's face, a fragment of the divine. In each other's faces we glimpse the face of the Beloved. In our own mirrors we see one of the many, many faces of the world. We are part of the beauty we seek.

Rags & Threads,
Wraps & Shawls

When the clothes of a robe do not
match the seasons, the flowers of
Spring and the Autumn tints, then
the whole effort is as futile as the dew.

Murasaki Shikibu
translated by Liza Dalby

As a little girl, I loved dolls and paper dolls, books from the United Nations with lovely watercolor sketches that showed the clothes, the "costumes" people wore around the world, the white skirts of the Greek men, the kimonos and saris and kilts and burnooses. In college my friends and I took to heart Thoreau's motto "Beware of enterprises that require new clothes" as we lived in blue jeans and big shirts; we were disdainful of our classmates who were interested in anything as superficial as clothes, while we were concerned with important issues like nonviolence and ecology. In my twenties I saw a sign tacked on the wall of a dancer's studio in Oakland that said: CLOTHES ARE THE AURA OF THE BODY MADE VISIBLE. And later still I learned of a Hasidic idea that garments are meant to extend manifestations of the soul.

Although I still appreciate Thoreau's critique of consumerism (now more necessary than ever), I also delight in the way clothes dance around my bones, the feeling of wearing a wonderful skirt in the wind, and walking down stairs to the ocean in flowing rayon or organic cotton pants.

From an early age we are aware that clothes can hide or reveal, accentuate or disguise. Clothing is connected to both sexuality and spirituality, lingerie and vestment. It is connected to collective dreams as well as to individual longings. Because dressing is silent, functional, and eloquent, clothing expresses our creative selves in subtle and private ways.

Textile artist Louise Todd Cope wrote a whole book on sleeves, exploring the creative possibilities in the cloth that envelops our arms. Questioning the necessity for sleeves always matching, since our arms are not always performing the same task, Cope once made a shirt for a musician with a trumpet sleeve for the left arm and a piano keyboard sleeve for the right. She writes, "I thoroughly, unabashedly love sleeves! I love their potential for magic, drama, and mystery!" She offers an alphabet of sleeves—angel, bishop, bracelet—and her reader learns that bagpipe sleeves were worn to "identify shepherds and tree pruners in the fourteenth century." Cope celebrates sleeves "as a theater stage on which the dance of our arms moves through space in life's daily gestures of joy, anger, celebration, whimsy, subservience, and yes, even fear."

Cope's sleeves—wide, narrow, puffed, pleated, gathered, adorned with pockets, words, buttons, and bells—suggest how clothing can open, focus, restrict, and dramatize our movements. Our clothing embraces and holds us; we hold our clothes around us. Garments move with us or against us, strengthen us, boost our spirits or "rub us the wrong way."

Like Cope, sometimes I am fascinated and delighted by the theater of clothes, especially for their intensity of color, the realities and possibilities of textures, their mood-changing properties, the roles our clothes play in our lives. At other times the whole business of dressing is just a balancing of practical considerations—the changeable Bay Area weather, the need to be able to wear something versatile as I negotiate through a day of many different tasks and emotional climates. For months at a time, especially when I'm busy or solitary or on a strict budget, I'm hardly interested in clothes at all. And when I am painting, I would be happy to live in white painter pants spattered with colors.

Then suddenly one day I admire the way a stranger or friend is dressed, or I'm passing a store window, and the whole pageant is fun again. Fun to dress up and explore a new possibility, to put on a hat or a bright pair of shoes or a shirt that smells new, to take the time to make a conversation between earrings and bracelet and socks.

Woven Histories

Clothing serves as protection, as expression of identity, as language, as decoration and delight, attraction and camouflage, uniform, chosen or imposed. Clothes reveal our personal history, describe our experience, define the time and place in which we live, announce our relationship to material things, our age, class. Clothing makes distinctions and separations, conveys respect. Through the centuries, women's marital status has been marked by aprons and sleeves, girdles and hats.

Clothing is shared at initiation rituals and clothing swaps, passed among family members; cloth itself has functioned as a form of "embodied wealth." Ancient Egyptians used linen as money.

Many cultures have woven their dreams and coded their myths into cloth. Clothes bring to life people in other times and places and make vivid the details of their daily routines. They also offer a route to our own memories. For some of us, the fads and fashions of our youth mark us as deeply as the music we listened to. In the constant parade of fashion, clothes show the subtle ways styles catch on and catch us by surprise, the ways we participate in our time.

Struggling to clean out my closet and pass on old clothes, I am reminded again how our clothes store our history, tell our stories. I complain to my filmmaker friend, Elizabeth, "How can I get rid of outdated beliefs if I can't even part with old sweaters?" She replies, "At eighty my mother still has her high school clothes. I've moved up and down the East Coast. Both these things have motivated me to simplify. I know my clothes function as a memory index. So now I keep a wardrobe video. As soon as my clothes start looking tired, I set up the video camera and film them. When I miss them, I know I can turn on the video."

I am curious about when and how we buy and recycle our clothes, the quantities of clothes so many of us have. The woman who cuts my hair says, "When I go shopping for clothes, I need certain colors. It's a very physical craving, like teething or hunger, a physical desire for certain tones. When I wear the wrong color, it's irritating, itchy like a mosquito bite. I have to take it off, if it's the wrong color for my mood, I can't wear it. For a long time I couldn't wear red. It felt too loud and big, too heavy. When I go on vacation, I bring a lot of clothes, because I never know what color a day is going to be. If I wake up and it's a blue day and I have red clothes, I'm in trouble."

Red rayon skirts, indigo jackets, beige linen, purple wool coats. Black velvet, apricot silk, brown corduroy. Texture and color meet in cloth to make a practical kind of magic, a private code of beauty. An African American playwright recalls the pleasure of seeing her East Indian mythology professor wear a different sari every day the whole semester. "I still remember a bright yellow sari with deep green detail. It was like the sun had walked in the room."

At one point in my life I imagined old beaus as various fabrics— luxurious green velour and serious unbleached muslin, blue denim, burgundy flannel. A friend laughed, said I was being generous. She imagined yellow polyester and a dirty gray T-shirt.

Reminiscing about old clothes, favorite sweaters, and work uniforms, many stories emerge. A woman notes that her father collected hats from around the world and another recalls her mother's suitcase filled with buttons and old fabrics. Growing up as the daughter of parents who ran a dry cleaning business in Kentucky, a woman remembers the necessity of looking "together" all the time. "Even to go to the grocery store our shirts had to be pressed." A younger brother observes that his middle school sister writes down what she wears to school every day, so she doesn't wear the same things too close together.

I remember the white-and-black, Aubrey Beardsley–inspired long print skirt I wore to give a speech for my high school senior English class more than I remember what I spoke about. Or the day six of us were sent home from junior high for wearing culottes to school. We spent an hour in the office arguing with the guidance counselor who told us we couldn't wear culottes to school because the word wasn't "in the dictionary."

A nurse revisits key periods in her life through her uniforms and costumes. As a young woman she was delighted by her designer navy uniform, "much more handsome than the army or air force uniforms." She later became a nurse and a belly dancer, both with their distinctive garb. Middle school students who dress very similarly to each other express outrage at the idea of school uniforms. It is amazing to see the ways people find to modify their uniforms. "My Catholic school classmates always found a way to express themselves, even if it meant wearing 'happy birthday' socks six months of the year," a woman reminisces.

Growing up in communist China, Jung Chang was highly sensitive to the subtle modifications that made the difference between fitting in and standing out. In her autobiography she recalls: "One day, from the open window, I saw Bing, a friend of mine, getting off his bicycle. My heart started to leap, and my face suddenly felt hot. I quickly checked in the windowpane. To look into a real mirror in public was to invite condemnation as a 'bourgeois element.' I was wearing a pink-and-white-checked jacket, a pattern that had just been allowed for young women's clothing . . . Because the range was so narrow, people were always looking for the tiniest variations. It was a real test of ingenuity to look different and attractive, and yet similar enough to everybody else so that nobody with an accusing finger could pinpoint what exactly was heretical."

If I were ever required to teach history or geography, I might approach the subject through the clothes that people wore in each era, in each environment. The Spanish shepherds near the Portuguese border wore straw raincoats; European women of the Bronze Age slipped into string skirts. The Egyptians dressed in linen tunics well suited to the Mediterranean climate. Investigating who made the clothes, what kinds of dyes were used, reveals much about the texture of daily life, the local economies and ecology, the trade routes and social hierarchies. Studying the clothes that have been forbidden and prescribed for men and women tells us much about the work each gender performed, the world each gender was supposed to inhabit. From bloomers to sports bras to leggings, athletic clothing has advanced women's freedom to participate in the world. The elegant and colorful kente cloth of West African chiefs, the cultures in which men wore flowing, flamboyant clothes, are startling contrasts to the austere way many American men dress.

I want to celebrate our instinct to fluff up our feathers, the creativity that we embody through our cloth and clothing. People all over the world have painted their bodies as a form of protection, magic, intention—the similarity in designs expressed as tattoos, as embroidery, even painted on houses. In *The Shining Cloth*, Victoria Rivers explores the ceremonial purposes and meanings that light-reflecting materials offer, suggesting that our love of these textiles is based on our instinctive attraction to the reflective surface of water as well as the radiance of the sun and moon. We contemporary folk, who live with the convenience of artificial light, don't remember our great dependence on the sun and our ancestors' reverence for its life-giving sustenance, the mysterious beauty of the moon, the power of its absence and its presence.

Gold and silver are certainly symbolic of power and wealth, but their multiple spiritual and ritual associations are an important part of their allure as ornament. East

Indian gods were reputed to wear golden garments; ancient Greeks and Persians were known for textural gold-worked clothing. Chinese rulers were buried in jade platelet shrouds stitched with precious metal; the Inca emperor was dressed in gold-embellished cloth. In societies in which people fear the evil eye and protect fertile women and vulnerable children from envious glances, it is believed that the white gleam of silver distracts and deflects negative attention.

In our time, the choices we make about simple and ornate decoration, tight and loose garments, sensual and efficient fabrics, flamboyant and understated styles, color and texture, are complex and fascinating expressions of soul and personality. Yet, through much of history, our clothing choices were limited by available materials as well as by occupation, class, and religious requirements.

An article by Mary Jean Jecklin in *Fiberarts* notes, "Before 1800, a rural Swede's choice of clothing was dictated more by age, civil status, marital status, community, seasons, holy days, and the church than by personal taste. Attire easily identified one's occupations. Styles were slow to change, and variations were resisted by the church, government, economics, laws, and the people themselves. Colors and designs were simpler than elsewhere in Europe. Nearly everything was carefully handmade in self-sufficient homes using coarse homespun thread, thick wool, linen, and fur. Set practices were followed for weaving, dyeing (with natural materials), styling, and sewing. Clothes were inherited and were sometimes more valuable than land."

A great variety of materials, processes, and skills go into the construction of our garments. There is something wonderful about the versatility of clothing that is composed out of large rectangles—sarongs and saris folded on shelves and in baskets. Ancient Greeks tied and draped homespun fabric into the day's costume. The high, hooded Tunisian burnoose, classic Berber dress, beautifully elaborated with gorgeous braiding along the collar, sleeves, and hood, is like a big army horse blanket. Cloth that functions as a "cloak by day and blanket by night" reminds us of the essential shelter that clothing provides. The daytime kilts of the Scottish soldiers unrolled to became their nighttime covers.

Across continents and cultures, stories about spinning and weaving illuminate the metaphoric and practical realities of making cloth. Back strap weavers, sitting with their weaving literally tied between their bodies and a tree, appear as if they are planted on the ground. Throughout the world, both horizontal and vertical looms evolved from this simple technology. West African weavers regarded weavin g as a divine gift and the loom as a sacred tool. When a weaver was leaving to go trading or to take a journey, he would take parts of his loom and throw them into the river rather than risk having them broken up for firewood while he was away!

In *Women's Work: The First 20,000 Years*, anthropologist Elizabeth Wayland Barber draws on archeology and linguistics, myth, craft, and economic history to document how much time and energy women devoted to textile work and how it complemented child rearing. Her attention to the daily lives of women, the interrelationships between language and clothing, and practical ways that clothing is adapted provides a whole new way to look at how we dress ourselves. Being a weaver as well as a scholar gives additional texture to her writing and depth to her research. Unlike many scholars, who study their subject from a distance, Barber takes a very hands-on approach; after setting up her loom to re-create a 2,800-year-old fragment of plaid wool found in the Austrian salt mines, she realized that she was having difficulty because she had reversed the warp and weft. It is through her weaving that she gains insight about the pattern of the tweed and the construction of the ancient cloth.

Given the perishability of cloth and the persistence of language, Barber also uses linguistic clues to study the interaction between cloth and culture. The words *robe* and *rob* came from the same root, because robes were taken as plunder. Both our habits of speech and our habits of dress take place below the level of thought. Subtle changes in speech and dress parallel each other so that a costume map can end up resembling a dialect map.

Many of our basic clothing styles date from the Bronze Age. The white tunic, red belt, and wool cloak Indo-European men wore was modified to allow horseback riding; trousers prevented chafing and the tunic was shortened to shirt length to allow for straddling the horse. Women wore simple tunics made from a soft plant fiber like linen or nettle, a belt, and a more roughly textured wool over-wrap. Barber notes, "Even the modern businesswoman who wears a white blouse, woolen skirt, and belt to work dresses in a barely changed later form of Bronze Age European clothing. After all, if it works well, why alter it? Fashionable details may come and go, but the fundamentals of how we clothe our bodies are remarkably conservative."

Conservative? We are used to the constant pulse of new styles, from the street to the couture houses, the fashion magazines and style sections reporting, proclaiming, hyping changes in colors and lengths, fit and silhouette. In the culture of marketing, we are always being offered something new. What a shock then to realize, if we consider the subject from a large enough point of view and generous enough expanse of time, it is really only a matter of a few details changing.

For all the time I have shopped and window-shopped, tried on clothes, flipped through the pages of magazines looking at clothes, and enjoyed exhibits of historical clothing, I have rarely considered why we wear what we wear, the history behind our garments, the way our ancestors' increasing technical sophistication informs the way we decorate ourselves.

The oldest known shirt to have survived into our time is a five-thousand-year-old linen garment from a First Dynasty Egyptian tomb, with finely pleated shoulders and sleeves, fringed at the neck. Strangely contemporary, this ancient shirt brings to life an unknown ancestor, speaks of the real history of the world. The wavelike pleats at the shoulders also speak to our connection with ocean waves and riverbeds, to the way humans abstract the natural world into our surface designs, the way we decorate ourselves with the forms of our landscapes. The shirt was discovered by Sir William Matthew Flinders Petrie, one of the first archaeologists to document the details of daily life as well as the more obvious splendors of the Egyptian tombs, in the early twentieth century. Nonetheless, the shirt languished for nearly sixty years, until two women museum curators found it while sorting through heaps of dirty "funerary rags" and recognized its significance.

What does it mean to the body to wear clothes from cloth that has been spun, woven, sewn, and decorated by someone you know? To wear cloth made from fibers that have been grown near one's house? I can recognize the taste of the tomatoes I grow and the tomatoes from my local farmers' market, but I don't have that same experience of localness when I dress. Cloth blessed by ancestors and divinities, cloth that is connected to the life cycle through the mythic stories of weaving and dyeing, has a weight and body and presence that is alive with meaning and memory.

Identity and Intention

Clothing, like food, is an element in our lives we constantly need to deal with, filled with routine and ritual. We designate and differentiate clothes to celebrate and grieve in, clothes for work and play, suits for swimming and sport. We claim favorite T-shirts, old sweaters, dancing shoes. Nightgowns hang out on door hooks. Drawers filled with pajamas. And underwear. "Can we write about underwear?" a few fifth graders ask me, giggling, when I propose clothes as a topic for today's writing workshop.

Descriptions of clothes in stories are used to suggest a character, a mood; they are props and metaphors, emblems and evidence of character. As any teenager knows, clothes are a language, a way of communicating that is poetic and prosaic, full of slang and odd quotations. Mothers of adolescents despair when their offspring care too much about clothes, or too little. Arguments about clothes between parents and teenagers carry so much power because they are about much more than the clothes. Such painful, poignant struggles to differentiate: "Even though I may look like you, I am not you." The great human need to belong and also to be distinct is played out through the theater of clothes. Years later, some of us remember the clothes we wanted, longed for, someone else had, or we never got. "When I was a young teenager," recalls quilter Nina Farrell, "my mother took me shopping at Hinks department store for my birthday. I was allowed a certain amount of money for dresses. I found one for the whole amount and my mother found five combined for the same amount. She tried and tried to convince me of the practicality of getting five and I tried them all on. The one dress was long, soft, purple velour and the most desirable garment I'd ever seen. I said no to the five dresses and my mother never went shopping with me again."

When we have many clothes and many choices of fabric and style, with relatively few rules, we can choose to be crisp and serious one day, more subtle or playful the next. Clothes offer immediate, and sometimes short-lived, transformation. A media consultant reports that no matter how you are feeling, you can put on clothes and change your mood. "You feel fat and ugly; you put on black silk—you become a water nymph. We're not really talking about the clothes. It is how you feel when you're in them."

How often, standing in front of a closet full of clothes, a woman complains that she doesn't have anything to wear, meaning she doesn't have anything that suits her now, today, that shows how she feels. Clothes amplify and transform who we are; they reflect the current mood and present us in the light in which we want to be seen.

As much as we emphasize dressing for others, our jobs and our mates, our friends, getting dressed is also about our relationship with self. The experience of clothes involves both looking at them from the outside and feeling them wrap around us, feeling ourselves held, held back, or contained within them. Putting on clothes after dancing or being in the forest, clothes that are loose or sensual, makes the skin happy. Wrapped in beauty, we feel more beautiful. A dramatic cloak, a black velvet bathrobe, a fine silk shirt is a delight for the one who wears it. Through color and cloth, we speak to ourselves as well as the world. After gum surgery, a woman spends the whole next day in her flannel nightgown; it's a way of comforting herself as well as communicating to her family, "I'm recuperating," even though she doesn't look or sound sick.

In my dreams I often see clothes I have never seen before, elaborate clothes I wish I could wear in "real life." I shop with my sister or pack suitcases in her old bedroom. I am wearing a turquoise party dress to a neighbor's wedding; I am talking to a mentor who dances superbly at seventy-five, and I am wearing a beautiful jade green jacket. Trying on costumes at a store that keeps odd hours, early and late, I am deciding to buy the clothes even if I don't attend the party. Recently I dreamed I was giving a woman three ethnic garments to repair like the beautiful ikat jacket dyed with indigo and safflower I found at a flea market twenty years ago. Clothes in our dreams may be about presenting an image, a facade, but they also express the many textures and qualities of our inner selves.

Our clothes are a borderland, a transition zone between our physical selves and the world, like a garden between the house and the street. Clothing can be nourishing and strengthening like a garden of vegetables, colorful like flowers. After all, until recently cloth has been made from plants and animals, a fact that is easy to forget in our ready-made world. And sometimes, in a room full of beautifully dressed people on a special occasion, in their "best threads," people do look like flowers in full bloom.

As a young girl alert to adult hypocrisy, I was very critical of the adults dressing up to go to synagogue in the fall for the High Holy Days, "like they cared about impressing each other more than they care about God." With all the melodrama of a sensitive adolescent, I railed against the superficiality of social-hall Judaism. I didn't understand then that there is a kind of respect involved in dressing up, that dressing up was not necessarily just about impressing others; it had the potential to be an act of devotion.

Coming of age in an era emphasizing "naturalism," I distrusted the artifice and elaborateness of the feminine styles available when I was growing up. We were not allowed to wear pants to school; my grandmothers wore gloves to go downtown. In college in the 1970s I embraced the casualness, the freedom to be comfortable, and the simplicity of my time. Reacting to the overemphasis on appearance, I wanted to be free of the fuss, the attention, the vanity table.

Now, in midlife, I have learned to appreciate what traditional cultures have long known about the value of dressing up. I can allow my need for comfort to coexist with a delight in refinement and decoration, a desire to wrap myself in beauty. As I have grown older and been able to choose which elements to add back into my life, I have a much greater appreciation for adornment, delight in playing with bold and subtle jewelry, colors and textures.

One of the last conversations I had with my grandmother was about clothes. She spoke about the women who dressed up at the nursing home, what for, and then elaborated on the red-and-white-checked two-piece outfit she had sewn for the High Holy Days in high school. She was always sewing. When I wear red, I think of her fondness for the color red, its bright song. A mail-order clothing catalogue reports that the "ancient Hebrew for 'alive' and 'red' is the same word."

All over the world, holidays and ceremonial days are opportunities for dressing up, putting on our "Sunday best," honoring ourselves and each other by the way we dress for the occasion. In certain spiritual traditions, students wear the same special clothes every time they take teachings.

In *Homo Aestheticus*, a study of art as a "biologically evolved aspect of human nature," anthropologist Ellen Dissanayake begins: "One thing Westerners notice with some puzzlement when visiting African universities is that even in oppressive heat the African staff members are dressed to perfection—the men, for example, wear three-piece suits, gold watches, shined shoes ... The Africans are exemplifying a belief that goes back to village society: care in grooming and dress manifests a civility and refinement that are considered to be fundamental human virtues. To witness sheer splendor and dignity of appearance, attend any public gathering in Africa and observe on men and women alike gorgeous costumes made of swatches of lace and bright printed or lacy fabric. The practice of dressing up as an aesthetic activity, the act of 'making oneself special,' continues to characterize the descendants of African people all over the world."

Clothes announce our intentions and help us remember our direction. When we wear certain clothes, our thoughts tend to travel certain roads. A California schoolteacher complains that when her children wear sandals and shorts, their minds are on vacation. Working at home, a friend reports that she still puts on a skirt to sit at her desk and talk to people across the country, making a distinction for herself between working and hanging out.

Our clothes also offer disguises, hiding our identity so we can move about the world in anonymity. Old Jewish stories speak of the Messiah as a beggar dressed in rags, appearing at the back of the synagogue, unnoticed by almost everyone. A textile collector recalls hearing about a tribal people who were ordered by the priests not to weave their traditional symbols into their garments. In resistance, they wove their symbols on the reverse side; the priests were none the wiser.

Clothes become part of ourselves, a second skin. Clothes wear out, get stained at the cuff by pomegranate seeds, torn by a kitten, spotted with lasagna. They are handed down to siblings and sent to relatives on the other side of the world. We spend so much time wrapped inside them it's not surprising that a part of us lingers when we step out of them. The everydayness of our lives is inscribed in our clothing.

Red Threads, Tassels & Buttons: Decoration & Ceremony

Clothing sings of absence and presence. When we see the clothes or the shoes of someone we know who has died, we are often startled by how much we miss them, the empty clothes an elegy, a lament, a protest. A woman recalls that when her cousin died, her grandmother insisted on buying new shoes to bury her grandson, "shoes that would carry the boy to God." In the 1990s, Griffin Dix collected 2,000 pairs of shoes to bring to the state Capitol building in Sacramento to protest the 5,500 lives lost to handguns in a single year, including that of his own son. These worn shoes, large and small, mute and utterly personal, are hauntingly effective at invoking the loss of real people, make visible the parade of deaths that we hear about over and over in the news.

Berkeley artist Sharon Siskin used shirts to memorialize people whose lives were claimed by the AIDS epidemic. In the early 1990s Siskin began running art workshops for people with AIDS. When the artist Ben Medina died, Siskin recalls that his brother offered her something of Ben's. "Initially, I thought he was going to give me one of Ben's paintings. Instead, I went over to the house, and he indicated there was a box of shirts I could choose from; I took a shirt that I remember Ben wearing a lot, a muscle shirt." Eventually Siskin brought the shirt to her studio and made a hanger for it out of bone, a vivid reminder that this shirt belonged to a person who had died. Reflecting on the Orthodox Jewish custom of covering the mirrors in the house when someone dies, she hung the shirt in front of a mirror and wrote the story of how the shirt came to her backward, so the writing is read in the mirror. Carving phrases in the mirror frame, attaching small objects to the bottom of the mirror, Siskin's piece honored her friend's life and death. As she continued her work with artists with AIDS, Siskin inherited more shirts, eventually displaying seven or eight of the shirt pieces in storefront windows in California and the Midwest. She included a pad of paper nearby for passersby to write comments. Although the work might be considered an installation, it also functions as an altar.

In its perishability, cloth reminds us of time and of the lives of those who inhabited it, of our own fragility. Clothes are mythic and ordinary. We are wrapped in cloth as soon as we are born; in many parts of the world babies are tied to their mothers' backs with embroidered cloth. Boys in southern China wear hats decorated with talismans and animal motifs to protect them from evil spirits. Traditionally, Orthodox Jewish men are buried with their prayer shawls. Throughout the world, humans have bundled and wrapped some of their most precious objects in cloth— sutras and scrolls, crystals wrapped in velvet and leather, sacred objects, rattles, drums, teachings. Wrapping is more than a practical way of carrying things as we move them; it marks boundaries and shows respect.

The artist Donna Henes used well-loved clothing from friends and the community to create a powerful and beautiful healing ritual for the patients and staff of the Manhattan Psychiatric Hospital. Henes tore the clothing she collected into strips and then, in collaboration with residents and staff of the hospital, knotted the cloth to the trees and fences around the site, 4,159 knots in honor of the 4,159 patients and staff. Each knot a note of love and concern. Collecting clothes and tying knots, Henes also collected stories. As she dressed the trees, Henes rearranged the landscape subtly, so people looked more closely; she was tying together the health of people with the health of the land. In the process, she bound together many strands as she considered the nature of healing, vision, suffering, and society's definitions of sanity.

Knots and tassels, fringes, beads, and buttons make visible an invitation to spirit, remind the wearer of his or her connection to the larger whole, to nature and God. Tying knots at healing waters is an ancient custom; Henes's practice of tying knots around trees echoes the rituals of women from Morocco to Armenia to northern Europe. In the Scottish Highlands, a piece of cloth dipped into the water of a holy well was used to wash an afflicted part of the body, then wrapped around a tree branch, the disintegration of the cloth symbolizing the disintegration of the ailment. Knotting the tassels at the end of a tallit, the Jewish prayer shawl, the tallit maker follows a specific number of wraps and ties, symbolizing the letters in God's name, connecting with the concept of God's oneness. Wrapped in the prayer shawl, one is reminded of God's love and protection.

On a more mundane level, a note card in a Mendocino gift shop declares, "Buttons and love hold the world together." Children love buttons; the button boxes on mothers' and grandmothers' bureaus evoke whole worlds. Buttons have been collected and traded, catalogued and used to adorn, communicate, and mark rank. A psychologist recalls that her mother and sister so admired a navy blue velvet English-cut jacket that a new beau had given her, that they both went out and bought identical jackets. Annoyed, she promptly changed the buttons to heart-shaped pearl buttons. A designer admits that she has spent more money replacing the buttons on a shirt with antique buttons than she spent on the shirt itself. When she passes on old clothes, she experiences a pang of regret about giving up the beautiful buttons, but she takes pleasure in knowing she is giving away something special.

I look at a photograph of an Egyptian marriage shawl embellished with buttons and tassels and red embroidered circles, cosmic wheels, and it looks extraordinarily beautiful to me. There is something wonderful about the way the buttons have found their way onto this ceremonial garment. The shawl is black as night and space; the small, bright buttons appear like planets or moons. Through handicraft the maker has communicated sacred information, making the inner body more visible, revealing subtle energetic patterns.

Throughout the world, embroidery has been practiced to protect the wearer and wrap him or her in symbolic and sacred information. Highly decorated areas include the necklines and cuffs, along the hems, and at vulnerable body parts. Geometric shapes, stars and spirals, flowers, birds, animals of the hunt as well as abstracted designs of nature decorate aprons, children's hats, men's robes, sleeves. For centuries, animals— camels, donkeys, horses, yaks—have also been dressed and decorated with embroidered regalia, protected with amulets and symbols. Red is the most frequently used color in tribal and peasant embroidery. In early Russian, red is synonymous with beauty. Linked with warriors and marriage, childbirth and youth, blood, birth, life, and death, red is both powerfully masculine and powerfully feminine. In the red sashes of Slavic men, in the red hoods of Micmac women, in red shawls and ritual clothing from India, in Chinese silk, red is vibrant, vital, and exhilarating.

We no longer embroider our clothes with red thread as insurance against ill-thinking neighbors, envious ghosts. Usually we go to stores and buy our coats and hats, our underwear and socks, our shirts and night-gowns without thinking about all the effort that went into their manu-facture. Certainly we have special clothes and talismanic jewelry. But to consider how little we are involved in the making of our garments is another way to think about how ready-made our whole lives have become. And although weaving and sewing our own clothing is not possible or practi-cal for most of us, we can become more aware of the daily and ceremonial value of cloth, layering this knowledge into the way we dress ourselves.

I am particularly charmed by the rituals that surround wedding clothing and gifts: the Danish bride who made her husband a shirt (and he carved an ironing board for her); the Hungarian grandmother who began embroidering sleeves for her granddaughter's dowry as soon as the girl was born; the East Indian grandmother who decorated her grand-daughter's handwoven wedding shawl with gold silk thread. Such care-fully stitched cloth offers a tender gesture to the future. In the making there is a sense of continuity, of stitching the generations together, so that the family continues beyond the life of any individual.

In many parts of Europe, people were buried in the shirt they wore at their wedding so that they could find their spouse in the next world. In fairy tales, shirts become important gifts because they are worn close to our hearts. Our cloth is a text, a story, a record that speaks intimately across time and place. Textiles communicate about the cultures they came from, the people who made them, the people who wore them. Ancient

Greek women wove storytelling cloths narrating the myths and deeds of their time. Hmong women who have made the journey from southeast Asian hill towns, to refugee camps, to modern American cities, tell the stories of their war-inscribed lives in brightly colored picture cloths.

≈≋≋≫

As a young woman, I had a housemate who was a weaver. Her loom inhabited the dining room. Her brightly colored yarns and threads, visible behind glass cupboard doors, were a pleasure to look at. Listening to the sound of the shuttles flying, watching her spend hours setting up the loom, I made a decision that weaving was one of the few art forms I wasn't interested in doing myself. Years later I have come to understand that there are many kinds of weaving in life, many activities that require the structure of a grid to allow the design to emerge, to support the repetition and variation that keeps the patterns alive.

Writing is also a kind of weaving, bringing together the threads of personal experience perpendicular to the threads of historical information. The tapestry of our lives includes many dreams and voices. Like weaving, language makes explicit certain patterns, creating threads of connection. The thread continues; the story becomes an ongoing warp.

Cloth becomes an image of wholeness. Following the threads of thought, we are reassured, satisfied, that out of all of these strands something coherent and useful emerges. Weaving, braiding, quilting, knitting provide us with metaphors for synthesis, for making something whole out of many parts, for making fabric strong enough to wrap around us and protect us.

As I continue to explore how it feels to wear and move in different kinds of garments, I notice how beautifully many dancers dress. I appreciate the dancer who announced that clothes are the aura of the body made visible. Do dancers love clothing because they know the body is also a wrapping, a cloak and veil that is woven of energy and substance, a beautiful and fragile wrap?

Clothing, like our faces and bodies, our houses, is partly a conscious creation, partly a collective dream. In its silence, it speaks of who we are and want to be, where we have been and what has formed us. A new mother seeing her small daughter wrapped in a beautiful blanket appreciates how the body is itself an envelope, the skin enclosing and embracing our muscles and organs, the body wrapping around the soul. Our clothes are a kind of skin, like tree bark, an envelope in which we envelop not words or messages, but our very selves.

Bone, Breath & Language:
In Praise of the Body

The Church says: The body is a sin.
Science says: The body is a machine.
Advertising says: The body is a business.
The body says: I am a fiesta.

Eduardo Galeano

In a Taoist text the student asks the teacher, "If my body is not my own, pray, whose is it?" and the teacher responds, "Your life is not your own. It is a blended harmony, entrusted to you by Heaven and Earth." This "blended harmony" offers an ardent reciprocity, a way to see our bodies as a home for the visible and invisible forces of the cosmos.

What would it mean to live as if the body were sacred? Even this question sounds awkward, because after all, when we talk about the body we are talking about us, ourselves, our cells. Asking, then, becomes the most tender, appreciative inquiry: what would it mean to live day to day knowing our bodies are beautiful? Beautiful in the way that anything that carries soul is beautiful?

A cardiac nurse says, "When someone dies, I open the window." And I breathe more fully. She adds, "We are our bodies until we are not our bodies."

Perhaps the body is a robe, a wonderfully woven garment that we

171

wear until we wear it out; perhaps it is a boat that carries the water in us through the larger waters. I want to move through these images lightly, open to possibilities that we are both much smaller and much larger than we can usually acknowledge in our daily lives.

More and more I appreciate the beauty of the body, not only the young bodies our culture has pronounced beautiful, but the beauty of this intricate vessel, this small boat navigating through oceans of air, mansion or music hall, sturdy old lighthouse, tiny radiant temple.

The Book of the Body

As we talk about the particulars of physical life, the details that give fragrance and texture to our days—grooming and illness, sports and sex and good food—something else emerges underneath the small talk. It is a song that speaks to the soulfulness of physical life, the marriage of body and soul, the most ongoing and long-lasting relationship we are offered. Our lives take shape and form as our bodies carry us through suffering and great joy. In and through our bodies we experience dancing and running, haircuts and dentist's appointments, back pain, headaches, favorite clothes, new shoes, many kinds of union. In the book of the body we are simultaneously experiencing and recording the story of our lives.

I love to hear people report the stories of their bodies, the details of maintenance—who brushed your hair, what you ate for breakfast yesterday and when you were in fifth grade, who massaged your feet. Listening to the parts of the body speak, we hear the stories of our lives from the inside. What is the book of the belly, the book of blood, the book of bones? What do your hands know—how to make piecrust, how to transplant a fern, how to comfort a child or draw with a twig?

What is the connection between our small bodies and this magnificent planet? How have you cherished and honored your body? Who told you the names of the trees? Who told you the names of your bones? Have you ever heard the stars? Does their fire run through your blood?

What is the body made of? The ancient elements. The same minerals we find in clay, in sand and mud, the stuff of earth. We share limbs, arms, and trunks with the trees. The dendrites of nerve cells and the bronchiole of the lung are both named for their resemblance to the branches of trees that extend in finer and finer lines from the central trunk, the main axis. Can you sense that your own spine is like a tree trunk, a ladder connecting ground and sky, heaven and earth? At times we look like moving trees, reaching arms from our trunks to the moon and the stars, gathering nourishment from the ground under our feet, our energetic roots.

Or perhaps we are vertical rivers, walking watersheds, all our tissues supported by elaborate systems of irrigation and drainage. We are made of water and thirsty for more. Water flows over the surface of the skin, the earth, across the land, on top of the land, inside the land, across the body, inside the body.

The heart is both ocean and lake, bounded like a lake, containing within itself the ebb and flow of the ocean. Fluid mysteries—water sings, and the body is the song. The body sings and water is its song. Our breath leaves moist traces, elusive like our footprints, our scent. We bathe ourselves in lakes and rivers, baste ourselves, our cells, in salt water. Our internal milieu evolved from the sea. We are salty, like seawater or bouillon, brothy; we are movement and moisture, thirsty and fluid, we carry the water in us. Our waters take many forms, become blood and saliva, bile, lymph, sweat, semen, tears. Our internal seas are as calm and turbulent, still and moving as any water we are drawn to in the world outside.

When a woman on the radio says that beneath and around every river is an invisible river, I wonder about the invisible body, the inner body, the shadows that follow us and enfold us, the light at the edge of the skin. How many bodies are there?

Our bodies take form from the places we live in, the streets we walk, the stories whispered by a grandmother as we drift to sleep. When my father was ill, I looked across the hospital bed at my sister's face and at his; we always thought I resembled him more, and I saw his wide eyelids in her face. Our bodies are the gift of our ancestors. We carry our parents and our children in our own bodies—in the genes, yes, of course, but also in the gestures and habits we observed and imitated in early life. We inherit not just their DNA and their features, but their physical patterns of communication, their dreams and attitudes toward survival. We carry stories in our ribs and our bellies that we don't even know we know. Our vocal inflections and breath patterns, the echo of an eyebrow, a frown, half remembered in your heart, your tears, your feet.

The book of the body, how far back does it go? We are fed and nourished not only by potatoes and carrots, chicken and rice, but by the conversation at the dinner table. Some of us ate resentment; others took in fear with our breakfast oatmeal. Our life substance is built from this legacy of food, from everything we digest, that almost can't help being both sweet and bitter. We belong to the accumulated experience of our flesh.

One way I have grown to appreciate the beauty of the body has been to study the body in a new way, letting knowledge amplify wonder, sensing my bones as I look at the diagrams of bones, allowing what I learn about our bodies to live in my body. Holding a model of the scapula, my hand experiences how it is the same size as the scapula and feels the way my three arm bones link shoulder and hand. I imagine the three-dimensional support of the shoulder blade, note similarities and differences between shoulder and hip, arm and leg, hand and foot.

Drawing and sculpting the body, even when I am not satisfied with what emerges on the page or with the clay, I also sense my own body in a new way. I become fascinated with looking at how the tendons in the neck move, and at the intersection of horizontal and vertical bones at the ankle. I am engaged by the places where we can see more of our bones; the inner body pushes out through the skin. Art-making amplifies the dialogue between looking out at the visible form and sensing into the inner spaces.

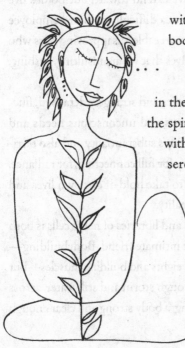

For years I have experimented with the way qualities move through the body, positive and negative. Fear moving through the body becomes terror in the chest, anxiety in the mind, panic in the skin along the calves. Joy moves up the spine and lights up the whole face from within. Harmony in the bones becomes serenity in the heart, radiance in the forehead. Feel the front in front of the back, feel the back in back of the front. Feel the currents and pulses, crosscurrents and spirals, dances of solidity, resistance and fluidity. Trust the needs and hungers of these strong, vulnerable body beings.

What on earth could be more important than knowing our own bodies, recognizing our bodies as part of nature? As we appreciate more fully the gifts of our own lives, we appreciate more deeply the beauty of all the animal and plant life we live among. The exchange of life force every time we eat, we breathe, we converse, we dance, we make love. What could be more beautiful than to know and celebrate the intricacies of interconnection? Every heartbeat massages the lungs; every breath massages the heart.

Our bodies contain many stories and mysteries, reports, sagas, journals of imprisonment and liberation. Terror and shame, sorrow and rage write their stories in our muscles and our organs, live in the chemical soup of our nervous systems, in the spaces between our bronchioles, our connective tissues. The attitudes we extend toward our bodies live in our bodies. When we treat the body as a difficult, awkward employee who can't follow instructions, or as a disagreeable, disapproving boss who keeps making new demands, it is ourselves that we are insulting, rushing, dishonoring, forgetting.

We are deeply attached to our bodies and strangely detached, fluctuating between self-conscious concerns and unconscious needs and conscious alignments, terrified of the body's substantiality and also terrified of our upcoming extinction. Hungry for full connection, for radiance, integration, beauty, intimacy, we yearn to take hold of our own lives and be at the center, to live in touch with reality.

This body with its thin skin walls and libraries of nerve cells is both self and friend, the oldest self, the most intimate friend. Bodybuilding—not only in the popular sense of lifting weights and building muscles—but constructing a vessel that carries us through storm and still water, across bridges we hardly knew we were crossing, a body strong and clear enough to carry more light, more beauty.

The Grammar of Bone

For many of us it is difficult to bring the experiences of our bodies into language. Can we discover the language of breath and skin, lung and liver? Experiences spiral through the body, as the body moves out and experiences the world. Listening for language, it's awkward even beginning to talk about "the body," because talking about the body as an object, separate from self, doesn't make sense.

Where is this mind? The brain is connected to the spine, the nervous system, the fluid that holds the organs. Nerve cells extend the mind through the meat of us, our flesh. Walking, I sense that intelligence lives in the whole body—the skin, the senses, the ankles, the toes. I feel like I belong to a long tradition of writers, walking to make sense, to marry the rhythm of thought with the rhythm of feet.

As I walk, I sense that the body speaks many languages—hand, heart, blood, belly, bone. Sometimes the question becomes not what do you know but *where* do you know? How do you hear? As if there were little ears all over the skin? When we walk, we are listening with our feet. When we touch, we are listening with our hands; when we look, we are listening with our eyes.

Like breath, language comes out of the body, comes into the body. Breath is sculpted into meaningful words by the vibrations of the vocal cords. We speak out of our mouths, the same place that chews and swallows, tastes sweet, sour, bitter, and salt. Our mouths taste familiar flavors and exotic ones, give voice to our names, our nouns, the syllables that allow us to tell each other about our lives. We whisper and shout, speak in tones and murmurs, choosing sounds and inflections that echo and amplify our own inner language.

I love the way the parts of the body live inside certain words.

Kneeling is literally bending one's knees, and in that gesture becomes a way to pray. *Language* is derived from *tongue*. And the tongue is the organ that enables us to speak, and is another word for language, as in *mother tongue*. *Courage* carries the word *heart* (*coeur, cor*) in its center, and reminds us that courage involves our emotional core; courage is a choice of body and soul. *Record*, to commit to heart, from the Latin *re-cord*. *Vertebrae* from the Latin *vertere*—to turn, one of my favorite roots, found in conversation and university and poetic verse. We *embrace* (from Latin *bracchium*, arm), encircling each other with our arms, and we wear bracelets that encircle our own arms. *Arm* (*ar*: fit, join) gives itself to making art and bearing arms.

Listening to the way we draw language from the body, we understand immediately how certain body parts become adapted as verbs: You *head* the committee, *mouth* the words, *eye* the crowd. From the shoulder to the thumb our upper limb moves out into the world. The soldiers *arm* themselves, you *shoulder* the responsibility, she *elbows* her way through the line, I *hand* him the letter and *thumb* through the manuscript.

As our bodies meet each other, we engage *face-to-face*, see *eye-to-eye*, dance *cheek-to-cheek*, walk *arm-in-arm*, have a *heart-to-heart* talk, go *toe-to-toe* or *head-to-head*, *shoulder-to-shoulder*. In these mirrored exchanges, we experience how proximity can be sweetly intimate or dangerously close. The nature of the interaction is indicated by which part is named.

The animal recognizes other animals. We claim eagle eyes and catlike grace, refer to our hands as paws and claws, horse around, bark at someone when they interrupt us, enjoy bear hugs. We get goose bumps and feel squirrelly. The animal metaphors carry wisdom and wildness, direct our attention to the way we move and behave, ask us to look at ourselves among the animals.

Gathering body idioms, I recognize something substantial about the way we draw from our bodies to make clear and effective metaphors. Based in gestures and sensations, these "figures of speech" are tendrils that reach into the tissue and flesh of everyday experience. They map our emotional geography, describe a poetics of knowing. We offer the poem "by heart." We make the gift ourselves—"handmade," it carries our spirit and our craft. In the presence of the beautiful, the amazing and immense, our bodies respond actively, immediately, undeniably. What is magnificent is breathtaking, what is delicious is mouthwatering. Sometimes beauty is eye-catching, sometimes heart-wrenching. Inspired, we breathe in the spirit of the mountain, the sunrise, the eclipse, a loved one's face.

Lively and honest, these body expressions summarize, illuminate, and locate the emotion in motion, condensing physical history into a few syllables. Naming these metaphors and idioms brings them to our attention. We begin to consider their origins and resonances. The idioms that come out of our bodies hold the immediacy of life. Yet, as they disappear into our language, we stop hearing the color and stories behind them, as well as the power and beauty of our language.

Some idioms are so visually vivid (from *head over heels*, to *off the top of my head*, to *she's all thumbs*) they ask to be illustrated by a great cartoonist who can convey their humor in a few lines. Others are like the tiniest of poems.

These body idioms lead into each other, taking us with them through a spiral of associations. Blood leads to bone, bone leads to "skin and bones," studying bone and skin brings attention to touch and then to hand. Blood is related etymologically to bless. Our blood cells are made inside the long bones of our legs. Bones endure; they symbolize both the immortal part of the human and the inner, invisible structure of the body. The backbone is synonymous with fortitude. Skeletons are figures of death in the popular imagination, but bones are also intimately connected to life—bones bleed when they are broken.

Shamans regarded knowing the names of bones as a form of power. When a dancer is moving from the bones, there is an effortlessness and clarity that makes her compelling to watch. When kids write about bones, they describe how our bones move us as we play sports, praise dancing bones, honest bones, and funny bones. A girl writes that she doesn't feel lonely because her bones are her friends. Do we move differently when we imagine our bones are friends with each other, our bones are our friends?

Our bones are covered by periosteum, which is a kind of skin. The organs are wrapped in membranes. The cells have walls of double membranes. The skin we see on the outside is just one of many membranes enclosing our substance. There are outsides to the insides, wraps within wraps.

We are intimate with our skin; we moisturize, massage, and decorate it. Our bones are a mystery, as unknown, invisible, important as our ancestors. Our knowledge of bone is based on intuition and imagination, occasional X-rays. Our skin announces our differences—age, health, sex, race; our bones emphasize our humanity.

"Skin and bones" is an idiom for being insubstantial, emaciated, the thinness of illness and poverty. Before we were so infatuated with thinness, *skinny* was not an adjective of appeal but of meagerness. The more accurate adjective would be *bony*, someone who is so thin his or her bones show through the skin. Except in rare moments like our own time, being either skinny or bony has not been a desirable state—to people whose lives and health were tied to their harvest, fat was the reserve needed to survive through lean seasons.

A woman who has struggled with her weight for many years

explores the distance between her skin and bones: "Jean and her bony self—bony lady. Now there's a phrase I haven't ever thought to apply to myself. And yet I have pretty much the same bones as those supermodels you see in the magazines, those ultra-thin women with their cheekbones and collarbones and hipbones thrusting out at you in ways my bedroom mirror has never experienced. No, you probably never think, 'Oh, that Jean. She's so bony.' But I'm every bit as bony as you. I just have more space between my skin and my bones than a lot of folks, so my boniness isn't the first thing you notice about me."

Skin sings to other skin. Skin to skin, limb to limb, the clothes fall away and we meet naked, in the words of poet Juan Ramón Jiménez, "as if we lived falling out of the skin into soul." Our skin is thinnest at the eyelids, lower belly, external genitals; thickest on the palms of the hand and soles of the feet. The feeling of one's lover's skin becomes one of the most precious intimacies.

To contemplate skin is to realize, as one physician said, that "the body is a boundary that isn't really a boundary." Like the cell membranes that surround and embrace each cell, our skin encloses us; like any edge, the skin stands between two realities, bringing us reports from the outer world, communicating about inner states. Skin blushes and glows, knows poison oak, sun rashes, scars that summarize and abbreviate our injuries into thin lines, our history into a few reddish inches. Skin knows heat and cold, the texture of cloth, the embrace of air, the way the breeze kisses us near the ocean.

Porous and waterproof, we sweat but we don't get wet in the rain or when we swim. In certain moments, it feels like our whole body drinks in the air through our skin. As a girl, I loved the way the air felt liquid through the open windows on car rides we took on humid summer Sunday afternoons to the eastern outskirts of Omaha. Is it so surprising that we take in the world not only through our eyes and ears but through our skin? Some of us are thin-skinned, metaphorically; we breathe through skin the way that frogs do, taking in the world through our skin, sensitive to currents and weather.

The owner of a boutique recalls that she was invited to a product demonstration for a line of natural skin-care products, and all the ingredients were edible—carrots, cucumber, strawberries, milk, honey. The manufacturer insisted that if a product is not edible, you shouldn't put it on your skin. It's another way of saying we breathe and drink in the world through our skin.

There is a kind of intelligence in our skin. Certain events "make our skin crawl" or give us goose bumps. Our skin changes when we are happy, with more breath, like cats when they relax and their fur becomes softer. The French have an expression, *bien dans ma peau*— "good in my own skin," inhabiting the body comfortably, fully in the envelope; it is an expression of wholeness, ease, and grace.

Skin and brain develop from exactly the same primitive cells. "Depending upon how you look at it, the skin is the outer surface of the brain, or the brain is the deepest layer of the skin," writes bodyworker Deane Juhan in *Job's Body*. "Surface and innermost core spring from the same mother tissue, and throughout the life of the organism they function as a single unit, divisible only by dissection or analytical abstraction.

Every touch initiates a variety of mental response, and nowhere along the line can I draw a sharp distinction between a periphery which purely responds as opposed to a central nervous system which purely thinks. My tactile experience is just as central to my thought processes as are language skills or categories of logic."

It may be an act of imagination to suggest that everything we see is looking back at us; it is the simple truth that whatever we touch, touches us. Touch, the poets insist, is the oldest language, the most urgent sense. Without touch, children can't survive.

I have always loved how we say "See you later" and "Keep in touch." *In touch*, as if it were a place where we could arrange to meet. Of all the senses, touch is the most immediately and intimately emotional. All the other senses are centralized around the face, but the sense of touch resides and travels throughout the skin. When we touch, we are touched, not just on the skin but thoroughly, through to the core. Touch can be subtle and sensitive, reassuring, and many kinds of sensual.

Just as sight is linked with knowledge, touch is linked with the emotional self. When we say that we are "touched deeply," we are talking about how much we feel. When we are irritated, we are *touchy*; *touching* is the word we use to describe a feeling that is precious, tender, dear. An archaic meaning of *touch* is "to play a stringed instrument."

The woman who cuts my hair insists she cuts by feel as much as by sight. As I sit in her chair, she describes teaching her daughter to make piecrust, talks about biscuit dough and bread and clay and hair. She started making pies when she was seven or eight. "You just have to feel how it is and watch how it turns out. If the dough is too dense and overworked, it's awful. You want the dough to be light and stretchy but not holding on to itself to be good. It's not like clay, not like bread, you don't work too hard, don't press into it. You need to be light, stay on the surface. With hair you do both, you stay on the surface and you go into it to feel the structure."

A bodyworker says, "My eyes are in my hands when I work." I feel the same way about making art. Painting is a dance between seeing and touching. I like to paint with twigs and sticks, break the familiarity of holding pencil or brush, twig to bone, eye, hand, move the paint around with a cloth, my fingers.

There is also a very tender connection between the hand and the heart. A third grade boy writes, "Hands like to hug and to hit," summarizing the hand's potential for tenderness and terror. The hands carry the messages of the heart through the arms out beyond our fingers, helping us touch, arrange, make, infusing our work with love. A man describes taking his sister to a surgeon and how he was "interpersonally dumb but his fingers glowed with intelligence. His fingers looked like Picasso fingers, brilliant intelligent fingers, like his hands were smarter than his head. He was like a post, except his hands shone."

The hands are messengers, translators giving voice to the body as much as our words give voice to our thoughts. We emphasize the activities of the hands, but they are also immensely receptive. Blinded at eight, Jacques Lusseyran describes educating himself to see through touch, and the receptivity involved in the process. "Touching the tomatoes in the garden, and really touching them, touching the walls of the house, the materials of the curtains or a clod of earth is surely seeing them as fully as eyes can see. But it is more than seeing them, it is tuning in on them and allowing the current they hold to connect with one's own, like electricity. To put it differently, this means an end of living in front of things and a beginning of living with them. Never mind if the words sound shocking, for this is love.

"You cannot keep your hands from loving what they have really felt, moving continually bearing down and finally detaching themselves, the last perhaps the most significant motion of all. Little by little, my hands discovered that objects were not rigidly bound within a mold. It was form they first came in contact with, form like a kernel. But around this kernel objects branched out in all directions.

"I could not touch the pear tree in the garden just by following the trunk with my fingers, then the branches, then the leaves, one at a time. That was only a beginning, for in the air, between the leaves, the pear tree still continued, and I had to move my hands from branch to branch to feel the currents running between them."

When children write about their hands, they describe hands that climb and grip, pet a cat's fur, become friends with dirt. They offer images of hands as restless as a hummingbird, as delicate as a ladybug's wing. A third grader exclaims, "My hands are like butterflies flying out of cocoons. My hands are leaves falling out of the trees." We write about what our hands look like, what our hands know, what our hands help us to do. I invite the students to draw their hands not by tracing them, perfectly, but by really looking at them. Watching a roomful of children looking closely at their own hands has to be one of the most beautiful things in the world!

After years of sketching hands in the margins of notebooks during meetings and lectures, I sign up for a sculpture class. Sculpting the hand, I notice veins and tendons, scars, the road map of lines etched into the palm, the fine scratching lines of skin. I start staring discreetly at the hands of people I have known for years, photographing the hands of a friend as he cleans a fish he caught, photographing the hands of a master printer. In my office I have a postcard of an Etruscan tomb sculpture picturing an ancient couple. Tenderness and love radiate from this couple but show most especially in their hands. They are facing the same direction, looking toward the same horizon. Both leaning back slightly, she is resting in the open circle of his arms. All four hands are portrayed mid-gesture, a mix of extension and active receptivity.

As much as I love words and faces, I love the languages of the hands, the handmade, the hand craft. Hands speak in the precious, precarious uttering we call prayer, extend the heart in mudras of protection and compassion, in blessings and crossing and supplication. The hand speaks eloquently not only in sign language but in handwriting, hand shakes and signals, gestures of impatience, farewell. Hands like flowers at the ends of our arms, starlike and shining with life, they are our most direct point of contact, of outreach. Dancing recently, I felt my hands holding invisible bowls and then become bowls of wind. At times our hands hold the cups of water we bring to our lips to refresh ourselves, at times our hands become the cup that, leaking, brings the water to our mouths. Our hands reach for light and love, hold stones and shells, the intangible qualities of air.

The hands offer a vocabulary of touch that is subtle, simple, and immense. The capacity of the hands to speak reminds us of the physical nature of language. In this journey we travel from language into bone, to skin, to touch, to hand, back to language. Bone and skin and touch, each contributing to make a most musical language. From the grammar of muscle and bone, the syntax of nerve and skin, the dialects of touch, the multiple languages of the body emerge.

Embodied Language

Attending to the structures of the body, there is so much beauty in the way we are built and the ways we build meaning. Exploring the roots of language, the histories that inform the words we use, in naming the bones, the muscles, the capacities of the nervous system, the fluid soup of chemicals bathing our spine, I am filled with gratitude. Studying the energy and structure of the body, the energy and structure of movement, the energy and structure of language, inspires more subtle awareness, increases connection and intention. There is purpose, intelligence, and beauty to everyday movement and everyday talk.

The embodiment of language is not something we are taught in school, but there is a root truth in language that comes from blood and bone, a sensuality in language that is a great source of pleasure, play, and wisdom. When language comes from the body, it becomes a bridge that connects us, almost like a material we use to build houses of words and houses of silence.

Alison Luterman begins a poem, "I love the truth the way I love picking blackberries," elaborating how "old truths hung too long on a bramble go soft and cobwebby / and truth picked too soon is full of acid." I realize that I love the body the way I love language. The way each is a form. The body seems tangible and substantial, language elusive and intangible, but sometimes it switches. Bones become visible from under the surface at wrist and ankle and knees, and language becomes transparent when we are most united with what we have to say.

Both our bodies and language are ways we give our beauty to each other—simple and straightforward or adorned and embellished with skill and delight. Perhaps, as the scientist Robin Dunbar suggests, language, and in particular gossip, developed as an aspect of grooming—casual, meticulous, playful. It offered a way for humans to bond and keep "in touch" as the social group became too large for members to groom each other personally. A strange and delightful idea.

Elegant speech in courtship and prayer is appreciated throughout the world. Delicate bold petitions, elaborate praises, outrageous spontaneous raps, vivid laments, and litanies of grief—so many of the heart's best poems are never written down. Spoken at times of great need and love, there are whole tapestries of words we will never read, because they were spoken between lovers, from the seeker to the Source, from the inner soul to the Great Soul. Offered from the heart in the moment, these songs are serious and sincere, a beautiful, transient, essential sweetness. Such eloquence reminds us of the beauty of living language, the honey of living story, the poetry that goes unnoticed in everyday life.

Language, like the body, is alive, expressing the soul, the self, the breath in phrase and gesture. Language becomes a dance, many dances. Dance becomes a language, many languages. To me the book of the body can't help but be about the body of language, spoken and written, chanted and sung. How many times did we make a shelter of good talk? A language of doors and windows? A language of light and shadow? A language of forgiveness?

The body is multiple, like language, with interpenetrating layers of visible and invisible beauty, weaving together form and energy, history and presence. I love the way tapestries emerge from the straight lines of the loom, music from the notes of the score, poetry from the energetic lines and small black marks, circles, half circles and zigzag straight lines of the alphabet, the human body from pictures of cells, X-rays of vertebrae, old Tantric diagrams, Chinese meridian charts, the anatomical drawings of Renaissance painters. From all these grids and maps something else emerges, full of curves and chemicals, the life force, glorious and spontaneous, always changing, finding form in our bodies, our expressions and utterances.

According to the Uruguayan writer Eduardo Galeano, the Guarani Indians used the word *ne'e* for both "word" and "soul" because they feel "those who lie or squander words betray the soul." And isn't it just as true that those who abuse or disrespect the body also betray the soul?

In the sacredness of both body and language, we sense their great commonality and realize how each can remind us of the other's beauty. It is not often in our rushed existence that we celebrate the preciousness of language and story, the preciousness of body and nature.

Finding our own language, like finding our own movement, is a journey, a labor that requires both work and play. Sometimes we have to stop making sense in order to find the real sense of what we have to say. In my creativity workshops, we gather words, making lists that move across sound and meaning: unwrap, unravel, temple, tremble, tassel, travel, ankle, uncle, shrug. Sometimes we specify physical words, emotional words, mental words, spiritual words, knowing that essential words like *blood* or *light* belong in all the categories; reading the word lists aloud becomes a kind of prayer. At a certain point we make phrases by combining words from the various lists. These combinations bring surprising images: bony prayers, coherent knuckles, joyful elbow, sad ankle, intelligent pelvis, holy mountain, magenta orgasm, articulate uterus, baskets of memory, bowls of soul. And more than anything else, these combinations suggest the beautiful coherence that the body offers, the movement of mind and muscle, the rhythms of wholeness that embrace us.

Remembering the Body's Song

May Swenson begins a poem, "Body my house / my horse, my hound." In my work with elementary school students, we consider that line as we hunt for metaphors for the whole body and its parts, the sense organs, the limbs. Children describe freckles as raindrops on dirt and cities on a map, eyes like cameras, arms like hammers and wings. These days, more often than not, the brain is like a computer—quick, complex, and efficient. Dissatisfied with this analogy, I wondered how else we could imagine the brain. I was excited to discover that the Nobel Prize–winning doctor Gerald Edelman suggests a better model, the intricately interconnected, abundant ecology of a jungle. The brain, like a jungle, is filled with layers of growth and life, color, sound and dynamic rhythms. Like the rest of the natural world, it is a messy place, characterized more by organic excess than by goal-directed economy and efficiency.

In the contrast between the jungle and the computer, we explore where and how we find metaphors, as well as hear something about the beauty of the life force, the interrelationship between chaos and order in nature and in the mind. Sometimes I feel like an anthropologist of the imagination; I can't anticipate when my students are going to be literal and concrete, and when they're going to leap into the immense metaphoric wilderness of the human imagination. The metaphors of the body come alive when we bring art and writing together. After working on a life-size drawing in a creativity workshop for adults, a participant describes her drawing: "I am a woman with wild blue hair, honeybees nest in my heart. I am standing on one foot rooted in the earth, the other foot poised in midair waiting for wisdom."

For many years I have reflected on a small poem by Eduardo Galeano:

> *The Church says: The body is a sin.*
> *Science says: The body is a machine.*
> *Advertising says: The body is a business.*
> *The body says: I am a fiesta.*

Galeano's poem is both useful and delightful, summarizing the vast belief systems that underlie the way we hold and experience our bodies. While it is only partly true, it gives us a way to appreciate how pervasive these views are and to consider others. To observe and study how these metaphors organize our experience reveals much about how we become exiled from the deep wisdom of life and from our own beauty. As we begin to swirl around in the assumptions, we realize we have inherited legacies of distrust for our bodies.

When the body has been treated as sin and machine and business, it is not so easy to hear the voice of the body proclaiming, "I am a fiesta." And often it is not so simple. To Galeano's celebratory declaration, I want to add other lines. "The body proclaims: I am a mystery. The body cries: I am a wilderness. The body insists: I am your university." Our bodies are ours no matter who wants to claim them.

The Church says: The body is a sin.

Our fear of the body—its flesh and weight, its hungers and desires, its pleasures and vulnerabilities—is insidiously mixed up with the deep distrust of women that has run through the major religions for centuries. While I am working with the Galeano poem, I dream that I am going to take a women's art class but it's canceled. So I enroll in a class called The Visual History of the Media in Medieval Times. I am questioning the instructor, a grad student, who insists that we write down exactly what he says, starting with the name of the course. As I copy the title, I hear the emphasis on "medieval times." In medieval times the church was the media, the source of narrative, information, and images. Religious paintings portray the sinfulness of humans and the compassion of Mary, suggest the mystery of God living through a human body.

Do I have to study the body in medieval times to understand the body in modern times, to copy down exactly what the grad student says? Is there some way I want the expert to tell me what to think, ignoring the wisdom of my own body? Or is the close and precise attention necessary? How can I, in my contemporary body, sense how earthy life was in the Middle Ages? Living with the intimate and continued presence of death—in childbirth, throughout childhood, through plagues—shaped people's feelings about their bodies in ways we can barely imagine.

I am seeking to understand body and beauty, body and wholeness, the wholeness that includes the exuberant body and the exhausted body, the body in pain, broken or ill, the young body and the aging body, the body in medieval times and the body in modern times. Even in sleep I am sorting through cultural delusions, prejudices, and old belief systems to come to some kind of knowing rooted in my own tissues and experiences.

Many religions have offered stories and images of heaven or transcendence detached from the complications and temptations of fleshly life. This distrust for the world of flesh and blood, skin and bone, gives rise to the need to control, criticize, and compare. Early Christians asked women to worship in veils because the allure of women's hair might distract men and even angels. Orthodox Jews require married women to shave their heads; Muslims fear that an uncovered woman's face ignites men's desires.

In one Taoist story, a beautiful Chinese woman seeks to travel to a powerful center of learning in search of wisdom. But when her teacher looks at her face and sees her beauty, he denies her permission to travel; such beauty is a distraction to others and a danger to herself. To prove the intensity and single-mindedness of her commitment, she heats oil in a wok and then pours in cold water so that hot liquid shoots out of the wok, burning her skin in several places. When she returns to her teacher, now marked by scars, he allows her to make her pilgrimage. Greatly disturbed by this story, I carried it to many people in my life, fascinated by the variety of their reactions. Perhaps for some this tale works as a story about the wholehearted commitment to enlightenment, the way beauty and ugliness are just roles to be worn lightly. Nonetheless, I ached when I heard it. For a human seeker, a woman, to scar her face to protect herself from the brutality of men is appalling.

For centuries women have been condemned for our sensuality, our allure, our desirability. In contemporary America sexuality has become so openly acknowledged (and advertised) it is everywhere; we don't live under the constant negation of desire. These days in the West, the word *sin* is more likely to be used to describe a rich dessert than a grave offense against God. Yet the legacy of the sinful body haunts us. The echo of shame opens us to the manipulations of advertising, the simplifications that allow us to treat the body as a machine and forget the body's wild, lively sacredness.

Science says: The body is a machine.

In our infatuation with technological progress, too often we forget the power and mystery of the life force. The idea that we can understand the body mechanically is reinforced by the way we frame our questions about how the body works. As soon as we are in the territory of *work*, leading with the interrogatory *how*, we are in the territory of explanations. How does the process of digestion work, how does the eye work, how does the nervous system work? It is not that these explanations are false, but that they are incomplete. They focus on function and performance. Healing the body, being moved by the beauty of a body we love, is something more.

The machines that we live with have rearranged our relationship to rhythm and time and provided us with a range of metaphors through which we describe our bodies. They offer a model of productivity that is incessant, relentless, and inescapably materialistic. Sometimes it seems like we are so inside the mechanistic model, it is difficult to see how it is like a veil between us and the world.

A gastroenterologist who moves comfortably between Western medicine and Chinese medicine is struck by how effective both systems are, as if he were fluent in two entirely different languages. Chinese medicine speaks in terms of balance and harmony, linking the organs with subtle emotional qualities; allopathic Western medicine is essentially mechanistic. As we recognize how many layers and levels there are to our bodies, we can appreciate the efficacy of diverse forms of medicine as well as metaphor, appreciate how different images invite and organize our thinking.

It seems like the body becomes more of a machine the more we look at machines. As new machines enter our lives, we borrow from their language to explain our experiences. The newspaper headline for a story about evolution announces, "Updating the Human Hard Drive." We talk about ourselves as being hardwired, we complain we need more memory. In the geek community, humans are called *wetware*, a word that refers to the juicy soup of the human brain and nervous systems.

What happens as we treat and symbolize our bodies as machines? Many stories suggest that when the machine becomes the model, it takes revenge. But perhaps the revenge is simply that we are sacrificing our bodies to a mechanistic life. As we lose appreciation for subtle layers of sensation and richness, our senses are dulled; we crave more extreme sensation to feel alive, more drugs to amp up and down.

It is astonishing how many different ways we have discovered to measure the body in the last hundred years—in the gym, in the diet industry, in the doctor's office. Using machines to monitor the body doesn't turn the body into a machine, something we sometimes forget when we start abbreviating complex processes into simple measurements. Our culture is not very good at valuing what cannot be measured. We have thankfully not been able to quantify the mysterious interrelationships between health and happiness, between daylight and mood, between body and soul, among beauty, soul, and body.

Thinking about how the body is not a machine has personally challenged me to enter into greater relationship with my own body, allowing both more emotional textures and subtle physical awareness, alerting me to my own rhythms of motion and emotion, rest and renewal. The body's changing rhythms include wide seasonal and daily cycles, personal pulses, steady beats and sharp accents. Like a Mayan festival with many different musicians playing throughout the village, the rhythms weave in and out of each other, creating a music of many layers and depths. Fluid rhythms, literally, from the flows and pulses of many kinds of time. Time, the medium our bodies dance in. Time in the mind behind the temples, time in the tides of the heart, time in the hungry belly, time in the patient feet.

The more we listen to our bodies, the more our bodies offer to teach us. Early on, many of us learn to ignore our bodies' rhythms. Taught to control and override our physical experience, we listen to and obey authorities instead. Too often we neglect and forget the body until she is shouting in agony, in hunger, in exhaustion, in loneliness, tension, and need.

"The body doesn't like to sit still," a friend says, but that is what many of us do through our school days and workdays, staying on task, not meandering, stretching. Yet, we are never really still; even when our limbs are quiet and we are only moving the fingers on a keyboard or talking into a headset, movement pulses through the inner body. Perhaps it is when we are most still or most joyfully moving that we begin to play with the paradox of motion and stillness.

Movement provides a wonderful laboratory in which to break the habits of the body as a machine. Watching animals and children stretch and sniff out new surfaces, roll around and bump into each other, I am struck by their ease, grace, and curiosity. When we see martial artists in slow motion, what looks like smooth movement turns out to be a continual adjusting and fine-tuning, moving in and out of balance, a lively turning away from and back to center.

Outreach and embrace, gesture and breath. The waves of the spine waking up, the arms articulate and free, fingers trembling sensing the air, movement radiating in all directions. Spirals and squares, lines and circles, the feet alive and active, calm and steady, listening to the ground. Experiment with rhythms of breath and pacing, walking, jumping, leaping, crouching, flexing, stretching. Walking backward, we interrupt the habit of relentless forward motion. Moving sideways like the lithe young Balinese dancers, we experience the ribs, the insides of the arms, the focus of the elbows.

Explore the movement in one limb. How many different directions, qualities, intentions, sources, motivate and animate an arm? Sliding out past the ribs in circles that emphasize the roundness of a joint, 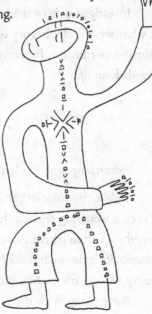 the inner arm brushes the breast and lung. Reach out from the shoulder or elbow or wrist; extend the arm from the back of the palm or the inner wrist. Sense how the arm is connected with the core; move one arm in relationship to the same leg or the opposite leg. Let the movement start in the belly or in the heels. Stretching out from the hand, or the elbow, or the inner shoulder can be gentle, decisive, angry, hopeful, curious, tender, receptive, patient, urgent. Our emotions shape and sculpt our movements, but our movements also shape, sculpt, and polish our emotions.

The body is not a machine. Our bodies humble us with their breathtakingly beautiful complexity and coherence. They overwhelm us with their capacity to hurt in some small place that we hardly notice most of the time. They amaze us with their capacity for exhilaration, ecstasy, exhaustion. We need rest, we need intimacy. We run late and we fall in love with people whom we can't get along with. Whether we find it in art or music or antiques or animals or the mountains or each other, we need beauty like we need food. It nourishes our spirits and feeds our souls. We are inspired and despairing, thirsty, out of breath, sweaty, lethargic, enraged, terrified, ecstatic. We cannot explain the body any more than we can explain beauty or healing or music or fire. The world comes in through our body's senses and we taste our lives. To savor the body's rhythms is to walk in beauty, to walk with uncertainty, acknowledge death in life.

Investigating how the body is not a machine takes us to the root of what we are, the beauty of the life force, the light and spirit that animates our breath. It becomes a way of seeing and praising what is sacred about life.

Advertising says: The body is a business.

Unlike the voice of the church, which often criticizes our bodily desires, advertising regards them as acceptable—provided we can buy something to fulfill them. Advertising exploits our physical and emotional hungers; its insistent and skillful images appeal to our desire for love and beauty, success, friendship, and purpose.

Advertising, with the meticulous attention to language formerly reserved for poetry and the promise of salvation once offered by religion, has a power we may complain about but rarely question. Jean Kilbourne, who has been studying cigarette, alcohol, and food ads for three decades, declares advertising a public health hazard, making clear that ads affect us where we live—in our bodies. Corporate advertising may be the largest single psychological project humans have engaged in, note psychologists Allen D. Kanner and Mary E. Gomes, yet Western psychology has ignored its impact. "We suggest that large-scale advertising is one of the main factors in American society that creates and maintains a peculiar form of narcissism ideally suited to consumerism."

The advertising media whisper incessantly that our own lives are not enough. How do we begin to know what nourishes us when we have been so skillfully convinced that we need something entirely different? How do we pay attention to our own images and dreams when we are being fed so many others?

Advertising's fluency in the language of images takes our eyes and removes them from the rest of our experience, takes our eyes out of the whole body they are embedded in and amplifies their connection to a certain kind of abstract imagination. When advertisers talk about "renting our eyeballs," it seems like an apt and accurate description of how the images we are looking at are driven deep into our brains and flesh.

When rooted in the body, in the landscape and the senses, our imaginations are not abstract, but very real and sensual. Because we have grown up in a culture where we learn early to separate our imaginations from our bodies and to treat our bodies as objects, many of us have to sense our way back to ourselves. Neglected, abused, the body still insists we experience ourselves. One movement of our time has been to reclaim the wholeness of body and soul, to see our selves in nature, as nature, and to extend respect and reverence for the body. Counter to that is our decreasing experience of physical life. We don't use our hands to make butter, make soap, hammer and weave, sow and harvest grain, mill flour, write out a poem for a friend's birthday. As life becomes more abstract, we are lost from our own sensation and knowing; consuming becomes a way to fill the void.

To critique the excesses of consumerism and the insidiousness of advertising is not to deny the pleasure of a new sweater or a pear-ginger muffin or a fine cream or a ski trip. The sensual soul enjoys the material world, but enjoying the material world isn't the same as buying enjoyment.

The speed of modern life, the stresses of overwork, the alienation from the natural world, are destructive to our health and well-being, our ability to appreciate the beauty in our own lives. Our bodies need and delight in rest, good food, time to hang out with fellow humans, to make things ourselves. With the loss of time for simple pleasures, we are more vulnerable to the culture of marketing. It takes time to cultivate friendship; it takes time to experience the dimensions and textures of our own lives. If we are always busy and rushed, we don't have the time to feel ourselves in the center of our lives.

Spend a week watching the messages that our media gives our minds, our bodies, our souls. The images of what a body is, what it looks like, what it is supposed to do block the experience of our own bodies until we have nothing but images relating to images. I want to free myself from the images we were fed at an early age—images of beauty and ugliness, images of what a young body is, of what an old body is, images of what a woman's body is, images of what a man's body's is, what a strong body is, what a vulnerable body is, what a healthy body is. I want to return to the invisible, unnameable beauty that gives birth to the body that lives and breathes and dies.

Celebrating the Body

After naming the thieves who have attempted to steal our bodies, Galeano gives the body the last word: "I am a fiesta." A celebration, a wonderful song, a dance of many rhythms and moods. The body is both the party and the gift we bring to the party. Perhaps the only real synonym for *body* is *life*. The task, then, becomes to stay alive to the truth that the body is fiesta and gift. Attending to the body is a primary way of attending to beauty.

We are just beginning to remember the dance of energy that creates the body. We move between substance and energy with limited understanding and great humility. The relationship between our interior and exterior, between the physical and the spiritual, is one of the great mysteries. Thin-skinned and trembling we enter the world, savor the flavors of experience.

As an experiment, I ask people for the most interesting or beautiful facts or aspects about their bodies. Responses come as quick short answers or more extended odes, the variety in the answers reflecting the range and depth of physical focus available to us: The eye. The hand. Breasts. Feet. That we give birth. That we heal. The way all the systems of the body work together. No matter how fat or skinny we are, skin still responds to touch. The way people have decorated their bodies from the beginning of time.

A cookbook writer is the first to celebrate body in

motion. Sharon says: "Movement, grace, the arms and legs and trunk, all the kinds of movement the body can make. That's what the body is made for. It's the best thing about having a body, being in a body. I think how beautiful plants are, but they move so slowly. That's the biggest sadness about plants." And then she adds, "You caught me on a day I did a lot of moving." Another echoes, "That we move, every single part of us moves; even when we feel stationary, we're moving in the rhythms of the cosmos. The body is made of movement."

A classical architect sensitive to rhythm and harmony answers, "The ear," and a voice coach celebrates the larynx. A quiet sculptor responds, "Transparency." A theologian says that we have orgasms in our sleep "no hands," celebrating the mysterious mental/physical nature of desire. A tattoo artist praises our diversity of shapes in limb and back.

A percussionist says, "I am in awe of the human voice—its ability to sing and laugh, the way it carries over distance. I like legs, too. And smiles—the way the whole face changes with a smile. But the ability of the voice to transmit emotion is magnificent."

"The most incredible aspect of the body is that through the body we can have heaven and earth. That's the most profound thing for me. That's why I work with the body," an acupuncturist states.

The responses become a poem in praise of the intimate details of our physical life. Engaging in this nonscientific survey, I realize how rarely we talk about what is delightful and magnificent in our own lives. What do you see when you look at the people you love? What do you sense when you feel your experience from the heart, bones, center of your life? What do you know when you align what is most beautiful and magnificent in you with the world? What inspires you about our substantiality, our fragility, our transient breathing bodies?

The more we learn about the eye, the ear, the hand, the heart, the muscles and bones, the skin, the processes of language and breath, the more we can appreciate the beauty of our bodies. The abundance of what we are given through our bodies is undeniable. Incarnation feels joyful. The body is indeed a fiesta. Our obsessive attempts to improve, impose, decide everything from our mind seem confused and sad and futile. We are made of and contain history and metaphor, tissues and dreams. Our bodies hold and include worlds as much as the world includes and holds our bodies.

I am fascinated by the harmony and dance between symmetry and asymmetry in our bodies, the singleness and doubleness, the relationship between individuality and community within a single body, the number of the parts—one heart, two lungs, one spine, two eyes. One mouth, two lips, one nose, two nostrils, two ears, two legs, two arms, the four of the hands and feet, the five of the fingers, twenty of all the digits. Our language offers pairs as well: skin and bones, blood and guts, flesh and blood, body and soul, heart and soul. The parts, the systems are separate and not separate from each other, just as we are separate and not separate from each other.

The visible body is one aspect of the body's beauty. The way we feel in our bodies, in our heads, where we are emotionally, announces itself through the forms our bodies take, the colors we wrap our bodies in, how we sit and walk and dance. Energy moves inside and around the body, our many bodies: the physical body animated by soul in every cell, the invisible body, the internal body, the body of emotion. Exquisite intimate physical intelligence guides us while we are receptive.

When we can celebrate the gift of life, we begin to have more perspective on the form and shape our self expresses. At such points the quest to take care of self, not to scorn or abuse or worship the body, becomes simple. Past the Romans and Christians, the glorification and the renunciation of the body that continues to play out in our time, past the obsession with body image that expresses itself in a zillion-dollar-a-year weight-loss industry and the exponential increase in plastic surgeries that offer to mask the aging processes, there is the possibility of a real relationship between body and soul. It becomes a choice, not a chore, to care for and cherish and love our physical form. Not imposing severe health regimes and austere diets, not rebelling, but tenderly caring for these small "mobile homes" with integrity and tenderness.

Life respects the immensity and magnificence of life. Awareness promotes appreciation. For some of us, the cherishing of our own bodies opens through a "close call" like an accident or illness. The death of some-one close to us brings us face-to-face with life's unpredictability and brev-ity. An injury or a chronic condition requires our attention, and while we may be annoyed that our routines are interrupted, we are forced to change. If we are observant, as we take care of ourselves, we discover what we had been too busy to notice. We gain more tenderness toward our suffering, more respect for our physical resilience and fragility. For others, the way is joyful—through an experience of birth or rebirth, through a day at the river or in the mountains, dancing or ice-skating or playing a great game of basketball. Unexpected moments of grace wake us up. Whether through life-changing events or a sequence of small moments, we are enlarged. We sense the generous friendship of the body and the soul.

Cups, Bowls & Baskets

I dream that I am living in a little town in the mountains. People are speaking several languages. Someone gives me a dictionary. Instead of hundreds of thousands of words there were only one thousand words but each word is in many languages and scripts: Russian and Persian, Sanskrit and Greek, Etruscan, Cherokee, Pomo, Navajo, Japanese, Spanish, languages from South America, Africa, and every language that has ever been spoken in the Middle East. The first word I look up is soul.

For years I have been inspired by images of the body as a vessel, an earthenware pot filled with varying qualities, elements, and energies, the bowl of soul. It is an image with echoes from many ancient cultures. When I read about cups, bowls, and baskets, I often apply what the writer is saying to our bodies.

Soetsu Yanagi, who pioneered a movement to appreciate the crafts of everyday life in twentieth-century Japan, emphasized the beauty of the natural, genuine, and simple. When Yanagi visited a Korean village where beautiful lathed wood objects were being made, he was astonished that the craftsmen used green wood. When he asked why they used material that would crack, the woodworker answered calmly, "What does it matter?" Inquiring further about the impracticality of using something that leaks, the woodworker replied, "Just mend it." Yanagi discovered that the cracked bowls were mended so artistically and beautifully that they seemed better than the originals.

Our bodies are like the humble Korean bowls Yanagi celebrates. The matter-of-fact naturalness, the beauty of what is strong and ordinary and useful that Yanagi identifies in the Korean bowls, offers us another way to look at our own forms. Our bodies are also strong and ordinary and useful, scarred and marked by what we have lived through, mended through our efforts, as well as through their own extraordinary ability to heal.

The word *vessel* suggests not only a container, but also a boat moving at sea, a starship traveling through space. A friend recalls that one of his most profound understandings of the body came out of a conversation with his father after his dad's first major surgery. "I recognized the body is the vehicle through which we experience everything we experience—joy, love, the emotions which we play like musical instruments in our bodies. It is the medium for all our joys—anything good that has ever happened to me in my entire life is because I have this body. It is important, for a moment it is magnificent. It is like it's the *Titanic*, it is a beautiful ship, it is not going to make it to the other shore. Realizing this brings to mind a poignant joy. My father is not someone to talk much about spiritual things, but out of this common humanness he and I met."

"Lord, help me. Because my boat is so small and your sea is so immense," a medieval French poet prays. "I am the vessel. The draught is God. And God is the thirsty one," Dag Hammarskjöld writes.

Sometimes the vessel becomes a lantern; a fine fierce fire warms us from within, shines through. The inner light announces itself through the outer form. The question then becomes: What feeds this light? What happens to this light in the presence of other lights? Echoing the French

medieval poet, I pray, "Lord, help me: because my fire is so small and
your galaxies are so immense. Teach me to be grateful for the beauty of
this fire, my life."

Walt Whitman wrote:

Was somebody asking to see the soul?
See your own shape and countenance, persons, substances, beasts,
the trees, the running rivers, the rocks and sands.

The double gaze opens into the world, into the self. Moment to
moment we are looking out, looking in, breathing out, breathing in. Our
task becomes simultaneously to attend more to the inner world and to
find ourselves in the world around us, like our ancestors, who knew that
memory is stored not only in our brains but in our landscapes. Often
we speak of inner life as the life of dreams and yearnings, intuitions and
emotions, the world of the spirit in contrast to the outer world of time
and taxes, deadlines and dishes. Inner life also suggests the inner life of
the body—muscle and bone marrow, vertebra and capillary, nerve cell
and lung tissue. Outer world is also tree root and river rock, anthill and
cloud. At some point the distinction between inner world and outer
world itself dissolves.

Years ago I worked with a dance teacher who took us outside to
dance under the sky, and we discovered that dancing outside is a special
ecstasy, to dance in and with nature. One night she invited us to dance
through the *o* in God. Another night she said we usually assume the soul
is a tiny element somewhere inside the body, a bright light in the mind or
in the heart. What if the soul is big, bigger than the body, and the body

rests inside the soul? As we dance through space,
extending feet, hands, elbows, ribs, we are
brushing up against our soul, moving
in an energetic circle that is our soul.
The body inside the soul! Everything
turns inside out. The soul becomes
as immense as the sky. Dancing with
each other, we are moving together in this
soulful air.

When we move from that image, it is
like taking a walk through a dense forest and
suddenly glimpsing the ocean through the
trees, or emerging into a wide meadow
that you had no idea was there. Turning a corner, the air is very sweet.

Every culture has words for
"soul." Different words for soul
open different windows into the
immensity, offering subtle fragrances, suggesting qualities of light, hint-
ing at different ways of understanding not just the soul but the body. The
Etruscan word for soul, *hinthial*, also means "image reflected in a mirror."
The Etruscans, like the ancient Egyptians and Chinese, believed that the
mirror held the soul of the person looking into it, and so to keep body
and soul together in the next world, they buried their dead with mirrors.
Hindus, Sufis, Kabbalists, ancient Egyptians map and name different
layers and levels of soul. There's a beautiful Kabbalistic idea that we receive
our fourth soul on the Sabbath.

Sometimes the soul is located in the head, sometimes in the heart,
sometimes in the liver, sometimes in the lining of the gallbladder. In the

spinal marrow, joints, and tongue. For a long time our ancestors thought the soul resided in the stomach; many Eastern traditions locate the soul in the belly. In early lore the diaphragm carried the power of thought and emotion. A contemporary doctor notes that everything between the heart and stomach is soulful. The soul's associations with specific organs is evocative but far from definitive. It reminds us how many different possibilities and visions our species has put forth. It evokes the abundance and variety of the soul's experience. It suggests the impossibility of fixing the soul definitely, defining and containing it completely. The whole body is filled with soul.

The dimensions of the soul are much larger than we can wrap our minds around and understand, but in our attempts we draw closer to our real nature as well as to the natural world. We develop many kinds of vision in the process. The eye looks out and in and beyond and sideways and through, and every kind of vision feeds the task. The eye of the imagination, attentive to dreams and metaphor; the eye of observation, alert to shadows and patterns of coherence; the eye of the heart, hungry for truth, are all necessary in this quest. The eye of the soul, Psyche's eye, sees in the dark and in the light, sees the light in the darkness, the shadows in the light, looks back and remembers, looks forward to encompass the long view.

It is one thing to think about the soul in a specific location, as a bright kernel, a radiant core, a vital primary intelligence, a dove, a tender trembling flame, another to investigate how the soul moves within us and through us, how the soul moves us into the world. Many languages, including Greek, Latin, Hebrew, and Arabic, link the soul with breath, the breath of life.

The close relationship between soul and breath sweeps across a landscape of time, what we were, what we are, what we are becoming moment to moment, breath after breath. The close relationship between soul and breath sings of the profound and delicate transitions and crossings that carry us into life and death. It is in our first breath that we join the human family, and it is in the gift of our last breath that we surrender our lives.

"The Eskimo word for 'to make poetry' is the word for 'to breathe.' It is a form of the word *anerca*, the soul, that which is eternal, the breath of life," writes Edmund Carpenter. "A poem is words infused with breath or spirit. 'Let me breathe of it,' says the poet-maker and then begins: 'One has put his poem in order on the threshold of the tongue.'" This connection between breath and soul and poetry links life and language, joining the unknowable interior with the abundant air we move through. When we breathe in, we draw a tiny piece of the infinite sky into the finite space of our lungs. As breath gives its energy to blood, we are continually nourished, enlivened, ignited.

Our English word *soul* with its tendrils into Saxon, German Dutch, Gothic goes back to a proto-Germanic word meaning "coming from the sea, belonging to the sea," because the sea was believed to be a stopping place of the soul before birth and after death. The soul's attraction to water, to moisture, is ancient and compelling. We are fluid creatures, breathing the steam, bathing in the living water, drinking in the wind. The soul belongs to the moisture of our blood and tissues, the vast oceans of water and air within and around us. The soul, like water, like breath, like music, mediates between gravity and levity, between stillness and motion, between life and death.

We live in a time in which it is easy to document the many ways we have lost touch with soul, lost touch with beauty. And yet, isn't our yearning for soul itself made up of soul, our yearning for beauty filled with the beauty we are yearning for?

"The world is so beautiful, and we forget it, like, every other second," a friend sighs as we walk in the early evening twilight. For some of us beauty is most available when we are outside in nature, at the ocean or admiring the diversity of leaf shapes—the fine fringed leaves of koa and acacia, the elephant ear. Others delight in what humans create: motorcycles and music, intricate architecture and simple sounds. The woman who cuts hair admires the beauty of a haircut, the man who roofs appreciates the beauty of a roofline. A woman who travels a great deal in her work says, "Returning home, I went to the farmers' market, and everything looked so gorgeous. I made soup for the whole winter. I'm not kidding. In the whole freezer there's no space left. When I saw those beautiful vegetables, I needed to make soup. That is how I came home." Sometimes we need to travel to faraway places to walk among people not speaking our language, and sometimes to sit at the base of a tree watching the light through the leaves.

In the soul's capacity to be intimate, with oneself and one's world, we sense that being with the Beloved takes infinite forms, many of them outside a theological language. At its root, intimacy speaks of inwardness; immensity is beyond measure, immeasurable. And it is the soul that bridges the distance.

Exploring intimacy and immensity in relationship to the soul opens up and mirrors the relationship between the personal soul and the larger sources of soul in the world. The Indian poet Kabir challenges:

Thinkers, listen, tell me what you know of that is not inside the soul?

Take a pitcher full of water and set it down on the water—
now it has water inside and water outside.

We are small bowls of soul, intimate jars for the immensity. Soul enters into form but surrounds form, too. The soul exists within and outside these vessels, our bodies. The soul's creativity shines forth in her capacity for relationship. The soul may be everywhere and in everything, but there is also a sweet particularity in the soul's friendships. Medieval women mystics wrote down dialogues between Love and the soul. Rumi inquires, "I am so small I can barely be seen. How can this great love be inside me?"

We have hardly begun to speak of the conversation between the soul and the heart, the soul and the body, the soul and the Beloved. The intimacy of the soul with the breath, with the life force, with a favorite piece of music, in a deeply focused task, are like a series of alliances that we rarely take the time to describe.

Perhaps the soul's friendships are better described in music than in language. Flute and drum, flute and violin, three cellos, a saxophone and a piano, harpsichord and voice, a chorus of voices, a string quartet. By suggesting a few of these combinations of instruments, we remember the conversation between the soul and the heart. These duets, trios, quartets describe the gorgeous and spontaneous alliances that the soul is always alive to.

Perhaps the dialogue of love and the soul is suggested by color combinations— pale pink and silver, the peach of certain roses, and the deep purple of Japanese iris, the red of blood oranges and the gold of the sun. Arranging small natural objects offers another way to make visible the way that the soul befriends whatever she engages with—put a white feather next to a pine cone, a candle next to a flower, and you can almost hear the soul speaking to the body, the soul befriending a fellow soul, the friendship of breath and body, soul and awareness. Perhaps it is because of the soul's affinity for song that she is sometimes described as a bird.

We also speak about broken hearts and lost souls, and in this language we hear ache and anguish, sharp pain and a diffuse gray confusion. We sense that the soul can wander away, be captured or stolen or compromised dramatically, or can suffer many small insults. The soul is part of us but also separate, apart, though we are lost without it, sometimes without knowing it. Soul sicknesses can be of the body or the mind—grief and despair as well as sudden physical shocks and long, slow illnesses that have the potential to call us home when we have become distant from ourselves. Maybe it is not our souls that get lost at all, but the rest of us that loses the soul. And sometimes we call the soul home in gentle whispers, sometimes shouting through noise that veils the soul's sweet voice.

And of course the broken heart, the lost soul, needs beauty, knows that beauty is healing, is helpful, even if there aren't ready-made prescriptions in exact dosages. Beauty is an essential medicine, a food and a language. Beauty speaks to the soul in a grammar of pattern and color, harmony and rhythm. Beauty offers solace and quickening, the plain coherence of unadorned truth.

Beauty, especially beauty in nature, wakes us up to a lively stillness, to wonder and awe, to a softening of the jaw, the belly, the worried forehead, soothing the heart. Rachel Carson wrote: "Those who dwell, as scientists or laymen, among the beauties and mysteries of the earth are never alone or weary of life. Whatever the vexations or concerns of their personal lives, their thought can find paths that lead to inner contentment and to renewed excitement in living. Those who contemplate the beauty of the earth find reserves of strength that will endure as long as life lasts. There is symbolic as well as actual beauty in the migration of the birds, the ebb and flow of the tides, the folded bud ready for the spring. There is something infinitely healing in the repeated refrains of nature—the assurance that dawn comes after night, and spring after the winter."

The psychotherapist Fran Dayan imagines flowers as she sits in her office with her clients: "Think of this. As I'm listening to a tale of isolation and hunger, I put a long blue delphinium behind her head and when she can see it without turning around she is cured and goes off to live the life she lives. Perhaps a bouquet of large outrageous peonies next to a woman languishing in doubt about whether to be single or married. Or cosmos at the feet of a man who can't get family and passion in the same prism."

Bringing these essential flowers into her office, Dayan puts beauty and psychology in the same prism, illuminating the purpose of the meeting. Rather than regarding her clients as a bundle of needs and troubles, or focusing on the problems at hand and then rushing through to fix them, Dayan envisions the flowers that symbolize her clients' wholeness, and sees her clients blossoming. She appreciates how these beautiful flowers offer us a secret source of wisdom, and she instructs us that tending to the soul of another person is like tending a garden. Her vision is creative and courageous enough to make a bridge between the anguished human heart and the radiant human soul.

In the beautiful, awkward words of someone who was not a native English speaker, "Never forget your soul and always giving it believing because it tells you the truth." The soul has an amazing capacity to know and perceive what is true, to intuit and understand patterns, to perceive movement beneath the various manifestations of reality. We can rely on our souls to tell the truth.

The curiosity of the soul has a deeply spiritual intent if we allow it to reveal and open us. The body is the soul's way of knowing life. Like art and life, body and soul create each other, belong to each other. When you honor one, you honor the other. When you dishonor one, you dishonor the other. You can't do something to one without doing something to the other. That's very old wisdom.

The soul blesses the body: isn't that what we need to remember now more than ever? Beyond the descriptions of the body as sinful and mechanical and commercial, beyond all the attempts to define and comprehend the soul, beyond our concepts and theories of the body-mind relationship, the soul gives light, depth, vision, and beauty to the body. The body's coherence and sensual substantiality, its beauty and sensitivity delight the soul. Perhaps the soul is that part of us which is eternal, perhaps it lives onward and outward, participating in ways we can only imagine, but here and now the soul lives in us, lives through us into the soul of the world.

The body is our boat and robe, vehicle and garment, it carries us and we wear it. The soul is a guest, a tenant, a friend, a traveler, inner navigator, the jewel and jeweler. The body and soul coexist between intricate layers of tissue, webs of energy. The soul loves subtlety and boldness, clarity and mystery, shyness and audacity—each of these qualities offering its own curriculum of beauty.

The soul finds itself through our bodies, our senses, through our hearts, through connection with other souls, through nature and the arts. When we begin to talk about what the soul yearns for, we are in the territory of poetry, the landscape of dreams and night oceans. When we talk about what the soul urges, the authority of the soul emerges. The soul's urgency and authority sing through the centuries. Even the fragments urge us to remember, to listen and live receptive to the soul's urgings and messages, whether they be cryptic or crystalline. The soul lives at the edges, soul at the center of everything.

"I will give you a musical note, sewn out of pure gold thread, from the heart of the ocean, wrapped in crystals and gems," a fourth grader writes with her whole self, and we step past our cynicism and are dazzled by the offering. We are made of song and soul as well as blood and bone, carbon and hydrogen, river water and tree branches. We are made of protein and fire, music and metaphor, breath and sky, muscle, mitochondria. We are made of what we eat and read and see and sing.

We find beauty in the intimate and the distant, the tiny and the immense, the small garden outside the back door and the majestic rain forest, the beautiful young people and the elders.

The ancient Greek harp player and the dark-ringleted psalmist king, the fourteenth-century Indian poet, the Japanese monk, the African praise singer, the Mayan shaman, the third graders writing about the wondering heart—all add their soulful voices to songs of praise and lament. An urban fifth grader writes:

> *my heart, the universe*
> *my mind, the stars*
> *my soul, the sun*
> *my blood, the moon*
> *my bones, the world*
> *my skin, the ocean*
> *my heart, the universe*

and it echoes with the simplicity and authority of an ancient chant.

We live in a reciprocal conversation with the world. There are so many ways to say this. The poet Ghalib declared, "It is the rose unfolding that creates the desire to see." Winston Churchill said, "We shape our buildings and then they shape us." And in *Anatomy of a Rose*, Sharman Apt Russell writes, "Flowers smell so good because insects smell so well," going on to describe how a honeybee might visit five hundred flowers in one foraging trip. Whatever we work on—music, creek restoration, teaching, gardening, cooking—works on us. It is always a conversation between the cook and the vegetables, the gardener and the plants, the artist and her materials, the bee and the flower, the body and the soul.

How do we honor this exchange, the generous reciprocity that sustains us? Traditional people dress up in beautiful clothes and offer food, say prayers and give thanks all the time. Praise, celebrate, honor, bless this moment. Acknowledge how much we are given in every moment. Praise "the sweet breathing of plants," who give us their oxygen, beauty, and nourishment. How can ecology not be a science of beauty?

A few months after my father died, I dreamed we were in a small chapel talking about beauty, and he said that the essence of beauty is "deep harmony." And in the dream it was clear that the harmony of beauty includes courage, truth, love, wisdom, and a profound respect for nature. My father, who collected clocks, grew orchids and opal basil, joked about serious things and was quietly compassionate, urged me to remember, to trust the wisdom of beauty. Waking up, I was struck that the messenger in the dream was not a Navajo medicine man or a Taoist sage or an ancient physician/philosopher but my Midwestern father, recently dead. I was profoundly reassured that the figure who came to close the circle, illuminate this simple and immense mystery, was so utterly familiar. The harmony of beauty. The beauty of harmony.

Beauty connects us to what is holy. In the book of blessings, which is always a book of beauty, we praise the senses, we praise the soul, and it is the senses praising the senses, the soul praising the soul.

Beauty lives in heirloom apple trees and seeds and the soft luxurious wool called cashmere, in so many things that I don't often think about in my world—in motorcycle dealerships and junkyards, in hospital corridors, the tender tentative steps of people walking after surgery, in the bird's-eye view out of the airplane of the line of the river and the patchwork quilt of field and forest, in the exchange of snow between the top of the mountain and the lowest floating clouds.

We are travelers passing through. We belong to this place, to this time. Growing into ourselves, we meet each other. The angel falling in love, falls into life. We find beauty in the garden and the forest. Let us begin to celebrate the beauty of the world.

Acknowledgments

Stories, friendship, and conversation are deeply beautiful to me, and over the course of writing this book I have treasured the conversations that stretched and sustained me. I am deeply grateful to Marty Barclay, Valerie Geller, Heidi Gundlach, and Georgia Schwimmer, whose words and wisdom are integral to this work.

Conversations with Christine Baron, Jane Bell, Pati Brown, Iesa Crowe, Sharon and Grant Elliot, Laurie Fox, Karen Freedman, Peter Gold, Linda Juratovac and Michael Philgen, Jeff Lerner, Norman Lippman, Greg O'Dea, Cayen Robertson, Linda Sanford, Sally Savitz, Judith Tannenbaum, and Nancy Thompson have also been of great benefit. A special nod to Maryann O'Sullivan for her careful and caring reading of the earliest chapters, to Kate Dodge for her intelligent heart, and to reference librarian and fellow writer and dreamer Richard Russo. Thanks to Emily Lyman for ongoing conversations that both circle around the particulars and focus on the essential qualities of beauty, and to Lynne Williams, who reminds me of a priestess from an ancient culture that deeply honors the feminine spirit with her ability to polish the soul as she attends to the face. My discussions with Irv Carlin, one of the first blind elementary school principals in the country, educated me and illuminated the nature of sight and inner vision in a real and personal way.

Certain people have been so important that there is no way I can articulate all my gratitude. Collaborating with Jeremy Griffith and Marian O'Brien over a nearly thirty-year period is both an ongoing gift and a given;

they have enabled me to travel farther and deeper than I could on my own. Jeremy Griffith's formidable intelligence and intuition have helped me to integrate thought, feeling and language. One thousand thanks to Marian O'Brien for her integrity, practical idealism, and dedication to beauty. My mother, Natalie Gendler, brings a sense of beauty into daily life through many small and elegant gestures; her discrimination, refinement, and intelligence inform all my work. My patiently impatient father, Irv Gendler, who did not live to see this book completed, was my ally, advocate and gentle critic, inspiring me to do my best work. I also want to acknowledge Beth Gendler and Rob Zisette, as well as Emily, Rachel, and Sam Zisette who have given me my eyes in many different ways.

In a day and age where the art of editing is increasingly endangered, I have been blessed by the skill of two superb wordsmiths. Many thanks to Deirdre Mullane and Renée Sedliar for their meticulous attention, clarity, and support. For careful reading and comments I am grateful to Shams Kairys, Jennifer Privateer, and Taly Ruttenberg. M. J. Bogatin's counsel enables me to work more effectively as a writer and artist. Thanks to Keith Whitaker for his contribution to the look of this book. I am deeply grateful to Jan Camp for her artistry and her competence and to Donna Stonecipher for her precise copyediting.

I want to express immense appreciation to my students and teachers, who are too numerous to thank individually, as well as the many people I have interviewed and talked to about the wisdom and power of beauty. I have been very much blessed to participate in several formal and informal learning communities. Teaching for many years through California Poets in the Schools I am continually reminded that though the beauty of the human imagination is not rare, it is precious and needs nurturing.

Paulus Berensohn's profound understanding of the relationship between craft and ecology and the urgency of beauty has been a great long distance inspiration as an artist and teacher. Thanks also to Richard Lewis for his gentle and generous encouragement and his beautiful work through the Touchstone Center for the Imagination.

My whole-hearted respect and appreciation to Eutony teacher Diana Sloat, who articulated the beauty of bone and reawakened my longtime interest in experiential anatomy, as well as Deb Marks and Peggy Dea for their great trust in the wisdom of our bodies.

Ed Schmookler and Michael Wagoner have patiently listened to the notes and followed the themes as the music unfolded; their company through this process has been an immense blessing.

When I first asked Richard Stangl, "Who gave you your eyes?" he talked about how much he doesn't see. His humility and kindness, his delight in looking at the world through many different lenses, adds immeasurably to my daily life. He underlines the world I see with his fresh perception and appreciation.

Notes

Invitation to Beauty

P. 6, James Hillman, *A Blue Fire* (New York: HarperCollins, 1989), 302.

P. 7, Ronald Shenk, "Navajo Healing," in *Psychological Perspectives* 19, no. 2 (Fall/Winter 1988): 226. Los Angeles, C. G. Jung Institute.

P. 8, Jung Chang, *Wild Swans: Three Daughters of China* (New York: Doubleday, 1991), 374.

Aphrodite's Gift

P. 15, Arthur Zajonc, *Catching the Light: The Entwined History of Light and Mind* (New York: Bantam Books, 1993), 2–3.

P. 18, Edward Hall, *An Anthropology of Everyday Life: An Autobiography* (New York: Doubleday, 1992), 188.

P. 18, Edmund Carpenter, *Oh, What a Blow That Phantom Gave Me!* (New York: Holt, Rinehart and Winston, 1972), 17.

P. 20, Bill Holm, *The Music of Failure* (Marshall, MN: Plains Press, 1985), 17.

P. 24, Robert Bly, ed., *The Winged Life: The Poetic Voice of Henry David Thoreau,* (San Francisco: Sierra Club Books, 1986), 79.

P. 30, Nell Dorr, *Mother and Child* (San Francisco: The Scrimshaw Press, 1972), inside front flap.

P. 31, Arthur Zajonc, ibid, 20.

Kinds of Light, Kind Darkness

P. 35, Patricia Lauber, *What Do You See and How Do You See It? Exploring Light, Color, and Vision* (New York: Crown Publishers, 1994), 5.

P. 41, Stuart Hample and Eric Marshall, *Children's Letters to God* (New York: Workman Publishing, 1991).

P. 41, Joan Erikson, *Wisdom and the Senses: The Way of Creativity* (New York: W. W. Norton & Company, 1988), 79.

P. 47, Linda Gregg, *The Sacraments of Desire* (St. Paul, MN: Graywolf Press, 1991), 10.

P. 49, Jacques Lusseyran, *And There Was Light* (New York: Parabola Books, 1987), 7, 11, 16, 17.

P. 52, Ibid, 312.

P. 52, Arthur Zajonc, *Catching the Light: The Entwined History of Light and Mind* (New York: Bantam Books, 1993), 224.

P. 53, John Daniel, "The Garden and the Field" in: *The Trail Home* (New York: Pantheon Books, 1992), 12.

Mirrors & Windows

P. 60, Edmund Carpenter, *Oh, What a Blow that Phantom Gave Me!* (New York: Holt, Rinehart and Winston, 1972), 120.

P. 69, Michael Ventura, "Beauty Resurrected," *Psychotherapy Networker*, January/February 2001.

Beauty Secrets, Love Stories

P. 81, Sylvia Ardyn Boone, *Radiance from the Waters: Ideals of Feminine Beauty in Mende Art* (New Haven: Yale University Press, 1986), 27.

P. 82, Nora Fisher, "To Adorn: At One with Life" in: *Mud, Mirror and Thread: Folk Traditions of Rural India* (Santa Fe: Museum of New Mexico Press, 1993), 25.

P. 94, Alice McLerran, *The Mountain That Loved a Bird* (Saxonville, MA: Picture Book Studio, 1991).

P. 96, Robert Sardello, *Love and the World: A Guide to Conscious Soul Practice* (Great Barrington, MA: Lindisfarne Books, 2001), 27.

Beauty & Other Forbidden Qualities

P. 103, Sonni Efon, "Tsunami of Eating Disorders Sweeps across Asia," *San Francisco Chronicle*, October 19, 1997.

P. 103, Andrew Higgins, "Prosperity Means More Chinese Well-Fed: Panic Time," *San Francisco Chronicle*, November 16, 1997.

P. 104, James Wolcott, "U. S. Confidential," *Vanity Fair*, June 2002.

P. 104, Blake More, "Starved for Perfection," *Yoga Journal*, May/June 1998.

P. 110, Louis Menand, "What Comes Naturally," *The New Yorker*, November 25, 2002, 99–100.

P. 114, Janet Fletcher, "A Haven for Butterflies," *San Francisco Chronicle*, May 19, 1999.

P. 114, David Roche, personal interview, June 1997.

P. 119, Carla Needleman, *The Work of Craft* (New York: Alfred A. Knopf, 1979), 52.

P. 120, Leonard Koren, *Wabi-Sabi for Artists, Designers, Poets & Philosophers* (Berkeley: Stone Bridge Press, 1994), 50–51.

P. 120, Joanne Gitlin, "Couture *Kampf*: Adventures in the Rag Trade," *East Bay Express*, March 1999.

Faces & Masks

P. 124, Alison Luterman, "The Grandmother Nose Poem," 2006.

P. 125, Kathy Peiss, *Hope in a Jar* (New York: Henry Holt, 1998), 31.

P. 126, "David Mura" in Bill Moyers, ed., *The Language of Life* (New York: Doubleday, 1995), 314.

P. 127, Tim Beneke, interview with Alison Gopnik, *East Bay Express*, November 12, 1999.

P. 130, Bill Buford, "Delta Nights," *The New Yorker*, June 5, 2000.

P. 136, Anita Roddick, *Body and Soul* (New York: Crown, 1991), 15.

P. 140, Hildred Geertz foreword in: Judy Slattum and Paul Schraub, *Balinese Masks: Spirits of an Ancient Drama* (San Francisco: Chronicle Books, 1992), 8.

Rags & Threads, Wraps & Shawls

P. 148, Louise Todd Cope, *Sleeves: A Treasury of Ideas, Techniques and Patterns* (Penland, NC: Coat of Arms Press, 1988), 3.

P. 152, Jung Chang, *Wild Swans: Three Daughters of China* (New York: Doubleday, 1991), 393.

P. 154, Mary Jean Jecklin, "Swedish Folk Costumes Reflect History and Tradition," *Fiberarts*, March/April 2001, 19.

P. 155, Elizabeth Wayland Barber, *Women's Work: The First 20,000 Years: Women, Cloth and Society in Early Times* (New York: W. W. Norton & Company, 1994), 68.

P. 162, Ellen Dissanayake, *Homo Aestheticus: Where Art Comes From and Why* (Seattle: University of Washington Press, 1995), xi.

Bone, Breath & Language: In Praise of the Body

P. 182, Deane Juhan, *Job's Body* (Barrytown, NY: Station Hill Press, 1998), 35.

P. 184, Jacques Lusseyran, *And There Was Light* (New York: Parabola Books, 1987), 27–28.

P. 189, Eduardo Galeano, "Window on the Word (III)," *Walking Words*, translated by Mark Fried (New York: W. W. Norton & Company, 1993), 40.

P. 191, Eduardo Galeano, "Window on the Body," ibid, 151.

P. 199, Theodore Roszak, Mary E. Gomes, and Allen D. Kanner, eds., *Ecopsychology: Restoring the Earth, Healing the Mind* (San Francisco: Sierra Club Books, 1995), 80.

Cups, Bowls & Baskets

P. 207, Soetsu Yanagi, *The Unknown Craftsman: A Japanese Insight into Beauty* (New York: Kodansha International Ltd., 1972), 122.

P. 212, Edmund Carpenter, introduction in: *I Breathe a New Song: Poems of the Eskimo*, ed. Richard Lewis (New York: Simon & Schuster, 1971), 11.

P. 213, Robert Bly, *The Kabir Book: Forty-Four of the Ecstatic Poems of Kabir* (Boston: Beacon Press, 1977), 4.

P. 215, Rachel Carson, *The Sense of Wonder* (New York: Harper & Row, 1956).

List of Drawings

Invitation to Beauty

Aphrodite's Gift

Kinds of Light, Kind Darkness

Mirrors & Windows

Beauty Secrets, Love Stories

234

Further Reading

Michael Ableman, *From the Good Earth: A Celebration of Growing Food around the World* (New York: Harry N. Abrams, 1993).

Elizabeth Wayland Barber, *Women's Work: The First 20,000 Years: Women, Cloth and Society in Early Times* (New York: W. W. Norton & Company, 1994).

Sylvia Ardyn Boone, *Radiance from the Waters: Ideals of Feminine Beauty in Mende Art* (New Haven: Yale University Press, 1986).

Edmund Carpenter, *Oh, What a Blow That Phantom Gave Me!* (New York: Holt, Rinehart and Winston, 1972).

Jung Chang, *Wild Swans: Three Daughters of China* (New York: Doubleday, 1991).

Louise Todd Cope, *Sleeves: A Treasury of Ideas, Techniques and Patterns* (Penland, NC: Coat of Arms Press, 1988).

Ellen Dissanayake, *Homo Aestheticus: Where Art Comes From and Why* (Seattle: University of Washington Press, 1995).

Joan Erikson, *Wisdom and the Senses: The Way of Creativity* (New York: W. W. Norton & Company, 1988).

Nora Fisher, *Mud, Mirror and Thread: Folk Traditions of Rural India* (Santa Fe: Museum of New Mexico Press, 1993).

Eduardo Galeano, *Walking Words*, translated by Mark Fried (New York: Norton, 1993).

Peter Gold, *Navajo and Tibetan Sacred Wisdom: The Circle of the Spirit* (Rochester, VT: Inner Traditions, 1994).

Ben Goldberg, *The Mirror and Man*, (Charlottesville, VA: University Press of Virginia, 1985).

Edward Hall, *An Anthropology of Everyday Life: An Autobiography* (New York: Doubleday, 1992).

Bill Holm, *The Music of Failure* (Marshall, MN: Plains Press, 1985).

Deane Juhan, *Job's Body: A Handbook for Bodyworkers* (Barrytown, NY: Station Hill Press, 1998).

Jean Kilbourne, *Can't Buy My Love: How Advertising Changes the Way We Think and Feel* (New York: Touchstone, 1999).

Jacques Lusseyran, *And There Was Light* (New York: Parabola Books, 1987).

Corita Kent and Jan Stewart, *Learning by Heart: Teachings to Free the Creative Spirit* (New York: Bantam Books, 1992).

Patricia Monaghan, *O Mother Sun! A New View of the Cosmic Feminine* (Freedom, CA: The Crossing Press, 1994).

Elizabeth Murray, *Cultivating Sacred Space: Gardening for the Soul* (San Francisco, Pomegranate, 1997).

Carla Needleman, *The Work of Craft* (New York: Alfred A. Knopf, 1979).

Kathy Peiss, *Hope in a Jar* (New York: Henry Holt, 1998).

Judy Slattum and Paul Schraub, *Balinese Masks: Spirits of an Ancient Drama* (San Francisco: Chronicle Books, 1992).

Victoria Z. Rivers, *The Shining Cloth: Dress and Adornment That Glitter* (New York: Thames and Hudson, 1999).

Robert Sardello, *Love and the World: A Guide to Conscious Soul Practice* (Great Barrington, MA: Lindisfarne Books, 2001).

Soetsu Yanagi, *The Unknown Craftsman: A Japanese Insight into Beauty* (New York: Kodansha International Ltd., 1972).

Arthur Zajonc, *Catching the Light: The Entwined History of Light and Mind* (New York: Bantam Books, 1993).

Credits